Essential
Amsterdam

by George McDonald

Above: *brightly painted canal boats on Prinsengracht*

AAA Publishing
1000 AAA Drive, Heathrow, Florida 32746

Above: *tulips for sale at the Bloemenmarkt*

Front cover: *typical canalside architecture; sunflowers; tulip-seller in traditional costume*

Back cover: *Dutch cheeses*

This edition first published in 2001 by AAA Publishing, 1000 AAA Drive, Heathrow, FL 32746-5063 U.S.A.

Copyright © Automobile Association Developments Ltd 1998, 2000, 2003
Maps © Automobile Association Developments Ltd 1998

The contents of this publication are believed correct at the time of printing. Nevertheless, the publishers cannot accept responsibility for errors or omissions, nor for changes in details given. We are always grateful to readers who let us know of any errors or omissions they come across, and future printings will be updated accordingly.

Published by AAA Publishing in conjunction with The Automobile Association of Great Britain.

Written by George McDonald

Library of Congress Catalog Card Number: on file
ISBN 1–56251–869–0

Colour separation: Pace Colour, Southampton

Printed and bound in Italy by Printer Trento S.r.l.

A01088

Find out more about AAA Publishing and the wide range of services the AAA provides by visiting our web site at www.theaaa.com

The weather chart on **page 118** of this book is calibrated in °C. For conversion to °F simply use the following formula:

$$°F = 1.8 \times °C + 32$$

Contents

About this Book

KEY TO SYMBOLS

➕ map reference to the maps found in the What to See section

✉ address or location

☎ telephone number

🕐 opening times

🍴 restaurant or café on premises or near by

🚇 nearest underground train station

🚆 nearest overground train station

🚌 nearest bus/tram route (refers to tram unless otherwise stated)

🚢 ferry crossings and boat excursions

ℹ tourist information

♿ facilities for visitors with disabilities

✋ admission charge

↔ other places of interest near by

❓ other practical information

➤ indicates the page where you will find a fuller description

---

Essential _Amsterdam_ is divided into five sections to cover the most important aspects of your visit to Amsterdam.

Viewing Amsterdam pages 5–14
An introduction to Amsterdam by the author.
Amsterdam's Features
Essence of Amsterdam
The Shaping of Amsterdam
Peace and Quiet
Amsterdam's Famous

Top Ten pages 15–26
The author's choice of the Top Ten places to see in Amsterdam, each with practical information.

What to See pages 27–90
The two main areas of Amsterdam, each with its own brief introduction and an alphabetical listing of the main attractions.
Practical information
Snippets of 'Did you know...' information
6 suggested walks and tours
2 features

Where To... pages 91–116
Detailed listings of the best places to eat, stay, shop, take the children and be entertained.

Practical Matters pages 117–24
A highly visual section containing essential travel information.

Maps
All map references are to the individual maps found in the What to See section of this guide.
For example, Artis has the reference
➕ 41E2 – indicating the page on which the map is located and the grid square in which the zoo is to be found. A list of the maps that have been used in this travel guide can be found in the index.

Prices
Where appropriate, an indication of the cost of an establishment is given by € signs:
€€€ denotes higher prices, €€ denotes average prices, while € denotes lower charges.

Star Ratings
Most of the places described in this book have been given a separate rating:
✪✪✪ Do not miss
✪✪ Highly recommended
✪ Worth seeing

Viewing
Amsterdam

Above: clogs on display
*Below: bicycles play an essential
part in the city's lifestyle*

George McDonald's Amsterdam

Gezelligheid

This is an essential ingredient of an enjoyable visit to Amsterdam. You should be looking for it from the moment you arrive, and if you don't find any you just might have grounds for demanding your money back. Fortunately, lots of places in the city are *gezellig* – cosy, warm and welcoming in a typically Dutch way. You find *gezelligheid* in such places as convivial brown cafés (▶ 114), intimate restaurants, characterful hotels and even on crowded trams.

Taking the air at a canalside café terrace

Welcome below sea-level. If this is your first visit you have a special treat in store, because making the acquaintance of this beautiful and fascinating city is the stuff of which fond memories are made. My own feelings on moving here during the 1980s were a mixture of astonishment that such a place really did exist and pride that I had become part of it – I felt like telling all the tourists on those glass-topped tour boats nosing along the canals: 'I live here and, hey, I can take the boat tour whenever I want.'

If you've been here before, you already know something of this feeling, and now you have the chance to dig deeper. Amsterdam rewards those who want to get below the surface, to get closer to the life of the city and its people.

It's hard not to be seduced by seemingly endless rows of elegant, gabled 17th-century buildings, their images reflected in the canals. Many cities have stately buildings but not all know what to do with them. Amsterdam cherishes them and makes them the stage for its own vibrant and inventive lifestyle, thereby serving up the best of both worlds. You can have all the sonorous incantations of history, art and culture you can handle, and afterwards you can let your hair down and party till the sun comes up and it's time to start all over again.

Amsterdam's Features

Bicycles
There are 550,000 bicycles in the city; 50,000 are stolen every year and 10,000 are recovered from the canals.

Piles
The Royal Palace on the Dam stands on 13,659 wooden piles – a figure all Dutch schoolchildren learn.
The Concertgebouw was built on 2,186 wooden piles; in 1983 these were replaced by 400 metal tubes.

Geography
• Amsterdam stands on the southern shore of the IJsselmeer lake, formerly the Zuiderzee, 24km east of Holland's North Sea coast. It lies 3.3m below mean sea-level, and is protected from flooding by strong coastal and river dikes and an extensive drainage-canal network.
• Water forms one-tenth of the city's area – 20sq km out of 200.

Population
• The city has 725,000 inhabitants of whom more than a third are foreigners and members of ethnic minorities from 50 nationalities.
• There are 30,000 students, 9,000 heroin addicts, 7,000 prostitutes and 3,600 police officers.
• Around 9 million tourists visit annually.
• There are 2,400 registered houseboats.

Government
• Amsterdam is the political capital of the Netherlands, but Den Haag (The Hague) is the seat of government and the royal family's place of residence.

Canals
• There are 165 canals, with a total length of 75.5km, containing 2 million cu m of water.
• They are crossed by more than 1,200 bridges.
• Seventy canal boats carry 2.5 million tourists annually.
• Every day, between 7 and 8:30PM, 600,000cu m of fresh IJsselmeer water are pumped through the canals to flush them out.

Leisure
• Amsterdam has some 40 museums, 750 restaurants, 1,400 cafés and 10,500 shops.

Left: *bridge over historic waters – one of more than 1,200*
Below: *feeding pigeons on the Dam*

Essence of Amsterdam

Below: *Amsterdammers like the cycling life*

Amsterdam has two faces. First, there is the historic city, in particular its 17th-century Golden Age legacy, which you can see and touch all around you as you stroll the canalsides. There are thousands of protected monuments from this period, and if you can blot out the many contemporary distractions it's easy to imagine Rembrandt strolling there, sketchbook in hand. Then there is the modern city, which has become a byword for its famously – some would say excessively – tolerant and freewheeling lifestyle. It's a tale of two cities, but in Amsterdam it is always the best of times.

THE **10** ESSENTIALS

If you have only a short time to visit Amsterdam, or would like to get a really complete picture of the city, here are the essentials:

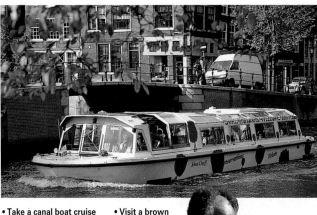

• **Take a canal boat cruise** (➤ 67), the best way to view this canal-threaded city and its gabled houses; it's even better after dark, when the canals are illuminated.

• **Rent a bicycle** and make a self-guided tour of the city the way Amsterdammers get around, or take our suggested tour (➤ 34).

• **Climb the Westerkerk tower** (➤ 26) for a great view over the *grachtengordel* (ring canals) and the Jordaan (➤ 54).

• **Visit the Rijksmuseum** to see Rembrandt's *The Night Watch*, the essence of the city's 17th-century Golden Age (➤ 22–23), and some of the museum's seven million other items.

• **Do the old centre walk** (➤ 64), which shows you there is more than the Red Light District to this part of town.

• **Have a drink or dine al fresco** at an outside terrace. De Jaren (➤ 94), beside the Amstel, has a great terrace for drinks; as has Wildschut (➤ 97) in Amsterdam South.

• **Visit a brown café**, one of the city's traditional, tobacco-stained bars, or a *proeflokaal*, an old gin-tasting house (➤ 114).

• **Listen to buskers** and watch other street performers at Leidseplein (➤ 20), the city's entertainment heart.

• **Stroll through Vondelpark** (➤ 25) in summer for the colour and animation that light up the park when the sun shines.

• **Travel on a tram** – Circle Tram 20 from Centraal Station (➤ 42) takes you to many of the city's top attractions.

Top: *taking a canal boat cruise*
Middle: *street musician*
Above: *a traditional brown café*
Opposite: *at home on a houseboat*

9

The Shaping of Amsterdam

c1200
Fishermen settle at the mouth of the Amstel.

c1270
A dam is built on the river at the village.

1300
Amsterdam granted a town charter.

1306
The wooden Oude Kerk is dedicated to St Nicholas; rebuilding in stone begins in 1334.

1345
Miracle of the Host; the city becomes a place of pilgrimage.

c1350
The city grows as a trade centre for beer and grain.

1395
The first town hall is built on the Dam.

1421
Amsterdam's first great fire.

1452
Second great fire. New law requires brick buildings.

1480
The city walls are built.

1514
The city is Holland's biggest, with 12,000 residents.

1519
Holland becomes part of Charles V's Catholic Spanish empire.

1535
Catholic rulers crush an Anabaptist revolt and execute its leaders.

1566–67
The first Calvinist church is built. Calvinists riot; the Duke of Alva executes thousands.

1576–78
Protestant Prince William of Orange (William the Silent) lays siege to the city. Calvinists take power in an event known as the *Alteratie* (Alteration), ► 38.

17th century
Amsterdam's Golden Age; it is the world's most important port.

The Prince of Orange, who led the Dutch rebellion against Spain

1602
The Dutch East India Company is founded. It collapses in 1799.

1611
Founding of the Amsterdam Stock Exchange.

1613
Work begins on Amsterdam's ring canals – Herengracht, Keizersgracht and Prinsengracht.

1632
Athenaeum Illustre, precursor of the Amsterdam University, is founded.

1642
Rembrandt paints *The Night Watch*.

1648
End of the war with Spain; Dutch independence. Work begins on a new town hall (now the Royal Palace) on the Dam.

1650
The city's population reaches 220,000.

1669
Rembrandt dies in poverty.

1697
Russia's Tsar Peter the Great studies ship-building in Amsterdam.

Opening of the North Sea Canal, 1876

1960s–70s
Amsterdam is Europe's 'hippie capital'. Anti-establishment 'Provos' win council seats in 1965.

1973
Van Gogh Museum opens.

1980
Amsterdam is named Holland's capital.

1990
The Van Gogh Centenary exhibition attracts almost one million visitors.

1992
Amsterdammers vote to eventually make the city centre car-free.

1999
A new wing opens at the Van Gogh Museum.

2000
Passenger Terminal Amsterdam, for ocean-going cruise vessels, opens.

2002
Wedding of Crown Prince Willem Alexander and Argentinian Máxima Zorreguieta in the Nieuwe Kerk.

1795
Amsterdam becomes capital of the pro-French Batavian Republic.

1806
Napoleon Bonaparte proclaims his brother Louis Napoleon King of the Netherlands, with Amsterdam as capital.

1813–14
After Napoleon's defeat, Prince William VI of Orange returns from exile and is crowned King William I.

1876
The Nordzee Kanaal (North Sea Canal) opens.

1928
Amsterdam hosts the Olympic Games.

1940–45
German occupation in World War II.

1941
Workers strike against deportation of the Jewish population.

1942–45
Anne Frank's family goes into hiding. Betrayed in 1944, Anne dies in a concentration camp in 1945.

1945 (May 5)
Canadian troops liberate the city.

1947
Diary of Anne Frank is published.

1948
Karel Appel co-founds the Cobra group (▶ 43).

1952
The Amsterdam–Rhine canal opens.

Elisabeth Robinson goes for gold at the 1928 Olympics

Peace & Quiet

There isn't much greenery in the heavily built-up inner city, though long rows of canalside elm trees soften the sharp urban contours. As you move out from the centre, green zones get thicker on the ground.

Canals

Underrated as a get-away-from-it-all resource, the city's canals are a haven of peace. A water bike (➤ 42) is a good way to experience this. You can cruise narrow side canals on these ungainly little vessels where the canal tour-boats cannot manoeuvre. If you're lucky, you'll even float smugly past a canalside traffic jam.

Gardens

Hidden from prying eyes, the courtyard gardens of the city's many *hofjes* (almshouses) are a good place to escape the maddening crowds. Best known is the Begijnhof (➤ 18), but it would be stretching a point to describe this popular tourist attraction as peaceful. Other, less well-advertised *hofjes* are scattered around town, particularly in the Jordaan (➤ 54), often with benches where you can take the weight off tour-worn feet. The same applies to gardens at such attractions as the Rijksmuseum (➤ 22–23), Museum Willet-Holthuysen (➤ 59) and Museum Van Loon (➤ 59).

A street artist soaks up atmosphere and lays down paint

Parks

Vondelpark, one of the world's most famous city parks (➤ 25), has grown up a little since it was the hippies' happy camping ground during the 1960s and '70s, but you can still catch the tang of fresh marijuana smoke in the air and have a high old time snacking on 'space cake'. Near by, frenetic Leidseplein (► 20) has a tiny scrap of green called Leidsebos, and Museumplein has been relandscaped, enhancing its garden-in-the-city appearance. Little Wertheimpark borders the botanical garden Hortus Botanicus (► 49), a block away from Artis Zoo (► 35).

A ring of parks, most with lakes or at least ponds, gives newer districts a garden-suburb character. In the east there's Oosterpark and Flevopark; in the centre and south Sarphatipark, Amstelpark (► 33) and Beatrixpark; and in the west Rembrandtpark, Erasmuspark and Sloterpark, which has a big lake for sailing and windsurfing.

If mere city parks are too constricted to contain you, head out to Amsterdamse Bos (► 33), a huge, wooded park that is nature on the city's doorstep.

The Amstel
At weekends and on warm, sunny evenings, Amsterdammers like nothing better than to cycle south along the green-fringed riverside to pretty Ouderkerk aan de Amstel village (► 85). You can do a stretch of this comfortably on foot.

The IJsselmeer
This large, freshwater lake (► 84), tamed remnant of the once menacing Zuiderzee, is a favourite place of respite. A car is the best way to get to the lakeside and find your own quiet spot, though a bike will do much the same job. You can easily get to such lakeside resorts as Marken, Volendam (► 88) and Hoorn (► 83) by bus or train, then walk a short way to quiet stretches of shoreline.

Below: *banking on the River Amstel*
Bottom: *the statue of poet and playwright Joost van den Vondel holds court in Vondelpark*

Amsterdam's Famous

Peter Stuyvesant (1592–1672)
The Dutch West India Company bought Manhattan Island (US) from the Manhattoes Indians in 1626 for 60 florins. Stuyvesant (▶ 42) was appointed governor of Nieuw Amsterdam, Holland's colony on the island, in 1646. He was a stern ruler, who opposed political and religious pluralism. In 1664 he surrendered Nieuw Amsterdam to the English, who renamed it New York.

Rembrandt (1606–69)

Born in Leiden, Rembrandt Harmenszoon van Rijn moved to Amsterdam in 1632, having already studied there, to further a career in painting, drawing and etching that would secure his reputation as one of the world's greatest artists. Unusually for Dutch painters at the time, he produced many canvases on historical and religious themes. Golden Age Amsterdam, though, was more concerned with portraiture and Rembrandt was constantly in demand, painting such classics as *The Anatomy Lesson of Dr Tulp* (1632), *The Night Watch* (1642) and *The Syndics of the Cloth Guild* (1662). Extravagance led to his bankruptcy in 1656. He continued to receive commissions, but died in poverty and obscurity.

Anne Frank (1929–45)

Born in Frankfurt-am-Main, Anne fled with her family to Amsterdam in 1933 to escape Nazi persecution of Germany's Jews. In July 1942, with Holland under German occupation, Anne's father hid his family in the rear annexe of a house on Prinsengracht (▶ 17 and 65), and she began keeping a diary of her experiences. Her dream was to become a famous writer after the war and she hoped to use the diary as a starting point. Betrayed in August 1944, Anne was sent to Bergen-Belsen concentration camp where she died in March 1945. Her father published *The Diary of Anne Frank* in 1947 and the book has since been translated into 55 languages.

Cruyff hits the dirt against Germany during the 1974 World Cup final

Johann Cruyff (1947–)

One of football's all-time greats, Johann Cruyff was player and captain with Ajax Amsterdam in the 1960s and '70s. He was point man in Ajax's highly mobile 'total football' style, which galvanized European soccer, earning Cruyff 11 Dutch league and cup medals and three European Cup championships, and propelling Holland to the 1974 World Cup final. With power and grace, he specialised in opening up opposing defences with balletic skill prior to driving home a knock-out blow.

Top Ten

Above: *the Begijnhof – an island of tranquillity in the heart of the city*
Right: *sax appeal on Leidseplein*

1
Amsterdams
Historisch Museum

*Step back in time at
Amsterdam's history
museum*

*A visit to this impressive museum will enrich your
understanding of the city's 750-year history,
adding useful insights to walks around town.*

Sequential displays of art, models, maps, weapons, household objects and other artefacts trace Amsterdam's development from fishing village, to trading post, pilgrimage centre, seapower and Golden Age capital; through wars, religious strife, decline and renewal, to today's vibrant metropolis. There are archaeological finds from the city's earliest days, the oldest city map, *Bird's Eye View of Amsterdam* by Cornelis Anthoniszoon (1538), four beautiful late 15th-century altar cushions depicting the *Miracle of the Host* in 1345, maps and globes by Johannes Blaeu, and the Schuttersgalerij (➤ 68), a corridor lined with Civic Guard paintings.

The Historical Museum opened in 1975 in the former Burgerweeshuis (City Orphanage), which took over the Sint-Luciënklooster, a 15th-century convent, after the 1578 Protestant Alteration. Architect Hendrick de Keyser added a new wing in 1598 and in 1632 his son Pieter built the Renaissance colonnade you see lining a courtyard shaded by a lime tree planted for Queen Wilhelmina's 1898 coronation. In 1634, the old convent was demolished and Jacob van Campen began construction of the main orphanage building. The museum has been renovated and uses interactive media to focus on the growth of Amsterdam and specific periods in its history.

Among many 17th-century Golden Age paintings, you can see the remains of Rembrandt's fire-damaged *The Anatomy Lesson of Dr Deijman*; Willem van de Velde the Younger's *The River IJ at Amsterdam*, showing a crowded harbour scene; Gerard de Lairesse's *The Continents Paying Homage to the Maid of Amsterdam*; and Hendrick Corneliszoon Vroom's *The Return to Amsterdam of the Second Expedition to the Indies*, showing four spice ships returning from the East Indies in 1599, an event that dramatically boosted the city's wealth.

✚ 40C3

✉ Kalverstraat 92,
Nieuwezijds
Voorburgwal 357, Sint
Luciënsteeg 27

☎ 523 1822

🕐 Mon–Fri 10–5, Sat–Sun
and pub hols 11–5.
Closed 1 Jan, 30 Apr,
25 Dec

🍴 David and Goliath Café
(€€)

🚌 1, 2, 4, 5, 9, 14, 16, 20,
24, 25

⛴ Museum Boat stop 5

♿ Very good

✋ Moderate

❓ Guided tours on
request; call ahead

16

2
Anne Frankhuis

Anne Frank kept her famous diary in a secret annexe of this canal house, where she and her family hid from Nazi persecution.

In July 1942, when the Germans began deporting Amsterdam's Jewish residents to concentration camps, Otto Frank, his wife and two daughters, and four friends, moved into a hiding place in the back of this house. Anne, who was 13, began recording her thoughts in a diary. For more than two years the eight *onderduikers* ('divers' – because they literally dived out of sight) lived in fear and nearly total silence until, in August 1944, an unknown informant betrayed them. Anne and her sister were sent to Bergen-Belsen, where both died of typhus early in 1945.

More than half a million visitors a year climb the narrow stairway and pass the revolving bookcase that conceals the entrance to the bare and gloomy refuge. Its emptiness adds poignancy to simple mementoes on the walls: magazine pictures of Anne's favourite actress, Deanna Durbin, and Britain's Princesses Elizabeth and Margaret; pencilled lines marking the children's growth; a map showing the Allied armies' advance from Normandy. Downstairs, the Anne Frank Foundation mounts exhibitions putting the diary into context, and next door at No 265, a wing for temporary exhibitions.

Anne hoped to publish a book about her experiences some day, using the diary as a basis. On 11 May 1944, she wrote: 'My greatest wish is to be a famous writer.' When Otto, the only survivor, returned after the war, a Dutch woman who had gathered up its scattered pages gave him Anne's diary. He published it in 1947 as *Het Achterhuis* (*The Annexe*). Since then, *The Diary of Anne Frank* has sold more than 13 million copies in some 55 languages.

✚ 40B4

✉ Prinsengracht 267

☎ 556 7100

🌐 Apr–Aug daily 9–9;
Sep–Mar daily 9–7.
Closed Yom Kippur

🍴 Café (€)

🚌 13, 14, 17, 20

⛴ Museum Boat stop 2

♿ None

✋ Moderate

❓ A 5-minute introductory film. Please note that the museum is quieter in the evening during the summer

Above: *queuing up to spend some time with Anne Frank (left)*

17

3
Begijnhof

The 'Huyten Huys', one of the city's two surviving wooden houses

A relic of Amsterdam's Catholic period, this secluded 14th-century refuge for pious women is an oasis of serenity in the heart of the city.

Begijnen (beguines) were not nuns but religious women who chose a less austere way of life, caring for poor and sick people. Most of their houses, with private gardens clustered around a tranquil walled courtyard, date from the 16th to the 18th century, all but one of the earlier wooden houses having succumbed to fire during the 15th century.

The exception is No 34, Het Huyten Huys (The Wooden House which dates from 1477). Restored in 1957 and oldest of the city's two surviving wooden houses (the other, 't Aepje at Zeedijk 1, dates from 1550), it is now the Begijnhof information centre. Look out for a courtyard beside Het Huyten Huys, whose walls are dotted with gable stones salvaged from demolished Begijnhof houses.

The church in the courtyard, built in 1419, was the beguines' church until Amsterdam's 1578 Protestant Alteration. Although called the Engelse Kerk (English Church), it is a Scottish Presbyterian church, having been donated to Scots' exiles in 1607. Piet Mondrian, co-founder of De Stijl movement, created its pulpit panels, and it is still in use as a venue for church music and recitals. The Calvinist authorities allowed the women to continue living in the Begijnhof; from 1671 until 1795 they worshipped secretly – it was an open secret – in the Mirakelkapel (Miracle Chapel) at No 31.

The last beguine died in 1971 and low-income female senior citizens now occupy the neat little houses. This is not a museum; it is their home. You should not enter after sunset or make noise or cause disturbance at any time.

✠ 40C3

✉ Gedempte Begijnensloot (at Spui)

🕐 Daily dawn–dusk

🚌 1, 2, 5

⛴ Museum Boat stop 4

♿ Good

✋ Free

↔ Amsterdams Historisch Museum (► 16)

❓ Guided tours with loud commentary not allowed

4
Koninklijk Paleis
(Royal Palace)

Constantijn Huygens called it the 'Eighth Wonder of the World', and this 17th-century structure remains the city's grandest secular building.

The Town Hall-turned-palace gives the Dam that royal touch

Jacob van Campen won the commission in 1648 to replace the Dam's dilapidated 14th-century town hall (Stadhuis) with a new one worthy of a prosperous city. He designed a vast, soberly classical stone exterior, a novel departure from the Dutch Renaissance style, and flaunted the city's wealth in the interior with lavish amounts of Italian marble. Completed in 1655, it rests on 13,659 wooden piles.

Royalty took over in 1808 when Louis Napoleon, whose brother, the French Emperor Napoleon Bonaparte, had made him King of the Netherlands two years earlier, chose the town hall for his palace and furnished it in Empire style. When the French left in 1813, the palace became the Amsterdam residence of the House of Orange and is still the country's official Royal Palace.

On the pediment overlooking the Dam, Flemish sculptor Artus Quellin (1609–98) carved a baroque hymn in stone to Amsterdam's maritime pre-eminence, showing figures symbolising the oceans paying the city homage, surmounted by sculptures of Prudence, Justice and Peace. The weathervane on the cupola takes the form of a Dutch sailing ship.

Symbolism is used prodigally inside, too. In the Vierschaar (Tribunal), magistrates pronounced death sentences watched over by images of Justice, Wisdom and Mercy. Atlas struggles to hold up the globe in the Burgerzaal (Citizen's Chamber) and maps inlaid on the marble floor depict Amsterdam as centre of the world. The Schepenzaal (Council Chamber), where the aldermen met, has a painting of *Moses the Lawgiver* by Ferdinand Bol, a pupil of Rembrandt's.

 40C3

 Dam

 620 4060

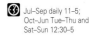 Jul–Sep daily 11–5; Oct–Jun Tue–Thu and Sat–Sun 12:30–5

1, 2, 4, 5, 9, 13, 14, 16, 17, 20, 24, 25

Museum Boat stop 1

 Good   Cheap

 Nieuwe Kerk (➤ 62)

5
Leidseplein

40B2

Café Américain (€€,
➤ 93); many
restaurants and cafés
(€–€€€)

1, 2, 5, 6, 7, 10, 20

Museum Boat stop 3

Vondelpark (➤ 25)

*What the city's liveliest square lacks in cool
sophistication – and it lacks a lot – it makes up
for in frenetic activity and tacky charm.*

In summer, sun-worshippers, people-watchers and
imbibers pack the tree-shaded café terraces rimming this
busy traffic intersection. Buskers work the crowd, most so
bad their victims gladly pay up to have them move along.
Throw in the city's biggest smoking coffee shop, a
plethora of restaurants, multi-screen cinemas, theatres and
clubs, and you have the ingredients of a hot and spicy,
non-stop entertainment centre.

A gateway in the 15th-century city wall once stood
here, at the end of the road from Leiden, where wagons
unloaded goods for the city. A row of 18th- and 19th-
century gabled houses on the north side are now cafés
and restaurants. The Stadsschouwburg (Municipal Theatre)
opened in 1894, and the American Hotel, Willem
Kromhout's extravagant mix of Venetian gothic and
Jugendstil, noted for its art deco Café Américain, in 1902.

A sculpture called *Adamant*, by Joost van Santen
(1986), in the Leidsebos (Leidse Wood) beside the
Singelgracht canal, commemorates 400 years of diamond
trading in Amsterdam. You can play open-air chess on
piazza-style Max Euweplein, an extension of Leidseplein,
and try your luck at the Holland Casino Amsterdam, the
city's only legal casino. Rederij Noord-Zuid canal boats
(➤ 67) and Canal Bike (➤ 42) have moorings on
Singelgracht, making getting to Leidseplein by water easy.

*Playing chess on the big
board at Max Euweplein*

6
Red Light District

It's misleading to think of this as no more than one big erogenous zone. The city's oldest quarter has some surprisingly characterful canalside scenery.

No beating about the bush in the Red Light District

Amsterdammers call this part of town De Wallen (The Walls), after the city walls that once stood here. Its two canals, Oudezijds Voorburgwal and Oudezijds Achterburgwal, are lined with lovely 16th- and 17th-century houses, many of them put to uses their Calvinist builders would find reprehensible.

The Red Light District centres most of the city's prostitution in one area where it can be controlled, and participants' health and safety more or less assured. Tourism, the international sex industry and Amsterdam's tolerant stance on drugs have transformed De Wallen, but people still live here, go shopping, walk the dog, dine out. Amid the sleaze are some good cafés and restaurants.

Few tourists visit to view the quaint gables, historic churches and second-hand bookshops, yet many tour the district not to sample its multifarious 'wares' but to experience a few harmless visual thrills before heading back to the real world. Even dedicated culture hounds will be hard put to miss the scantily clad women posing behind their red-fringed windows, knitting, reading or listening to their MP3 players while waiting for customers. Do not attempt to photograph the women – both they and their minders are likely to react strongly to this.

Their highly personal services complement a slew of 'live shows', peep-shows, massage parlours, video libraries, and specialised book, clothing and appliance shops. Ironically, the setting can be delightful at night, when colourful neon glows like Japanese lanterns on the inky canal surface.

➕ 41D4

✉ Between Warmoesstraat, Zeedijk, Nieuwmarkt, Kloveniersburgwal and Damstraat

🍴 Many choices (€–€€)

Ⓜ Nieuwmarkt

🚃 4, 9, 14, 16, 20, 24, 25

🔁 Koninklijk Paleis (► 19), Nieuwe Kerk (► 62), Oude Kerk (► 63)

❓ For a behind-the-scenes tour contact Rob van der Hulst Producties ✉ Zeedijk 34 ☎ 624 5720

7

Rijksmuseum

Holland's biggest museum gathers the best of the country's artistic and cultural heritage together under a single roof.

The State Museum lifts the lid on a thousand years of Dutch art and culture

Only a fraction of the museum's seven million items is on display, ranging from the world's most important array of Dutch Golden Age art, through beautifully detailed model sailing ships to 18th-century doll's houses. It fills 260 rooms encompassing five departments – Painting, Print Room, Dutch History, Asiatic Art, Sculpture and Decorative Arts – and presents you with an awesome cultural feast. Petrus Josephus Hubertus Cuypers (1827–1921), a Catholic, designed the building as a neo-Renaissance palace suitable for housing the creative genius of a Protestant nation. As construction proceeded between 1865 and 1885, he slipped in neo-gothic elements, causing King William III to refuse to enter what he called 'that monastery'.

Rembrandt's masterpiece *The Company of Captain Frans Banning Cocq and Lieutenant Willem van Ruytenburch*, better known as *The Night Watch* (1642), has a room to itself. Repaired after having been slashed in 1975, it shows smartly uniformed Amsterdam militiamen getting ready for a patrol. Despite its popular title, the painting depicts a daytime scene, as was shown when restoration removed centuries of grime to reveal sunlight glinting on the militiamen's arms and accoutrements.

Among 19 other Rembrandts are the tender *Jewish Bride* (c1665); *The Syndics of the Cloth Guild* (1662), painted after his 1656 bankruptcy; and two self-portraits, one showing a brash and successful artist in his twenties, the other a worn and saddened 55-year-old dressed as the Apostle Paul.

The register of emblematic paintings seems unending. A brief list of the most famous includes: Jan Steen's *The Feast of St Nicholas* (c1660–5); Frans Hals's *The Company of Captain Rainier Raeal* (1637); Willem van de Velde the Elder's *The Battle of the Downs* (1639); Pieter Saenredam's *Amsterdam Town Hall* (1657); Hendrick Averkamp's *Winter Landscape with Ice-Skaters* (undated);

✚ 40B1

✉ Stadhouderskade 42

☎ 674 7047

🕐 Daily 10–5. Closed 1 Jan

🍴 Café Cuijpers (€€)

🚌 2, 5, 6, 7, 10, 20

🚤 Museum Boat stop 3

♿ Very good

✋ Expensive (Garden free)

↔ Stedelijk Museum (➤ 71), Van Gogh Museum (➤ 24), Vondelpark (➤ 25)

❓ ARIA touch-screen virtual tour; audio-tour

Jacob van Ruisdael's *Windmill at Wijk bij Duurstede* (c1665); and Karel Dujardin's *The Regents of the Spinhuis and New Workhouse* (1669). Jan Vermeer (1632–75) is represented by four works: *The Milkmaid* (1658), *The Little Street* (c1658), *The Love Letter* (c1670) and *Woman Reading a Letter* (1662–63). Then there are later Dutch artists of The Hague School and the Amsterdam Impressionists; international artists such as Fra Angelico, Tiepolo, Goya, Rubens and Van Dyck; as well as medieval and religious art.

The Dutch history section covers the period from the Middle Ages to the present century; the china and porcelain collection includes a magnificent assortment of blue and polychrome delftware; and the Rijksprentenkabinet displays some of the museum's hoard of prints and engravings. Asian and Islamic art occupy the South Wing (entrance at Hobbemastraat 19), designed by Pieter Cuyper's son Jos and built between 1906 and 1909.

The Rijksmuseum's garden, a little-known attraction, is a restful scene of well-tended flower-beds, fountains and summerhouses, and the setting for a collection of sculptural fragments from around Holland, including the Fragments Building, a mishmash of pilasters, gables, lion masks and festoons from demolished monuments.

Rembrandt's masterpiece, The Night Watch, is star of the show

23

8
Van Gogh Museum

40B1

Paulus Potterstraat 7

570 5200

Daily 10–6. Closed 1 Jan

Self-service restaurant
(€–€€)

2, 3, 5, 12, 16, 20

Museum Boat stop 3

Excellent

Expensive

Rijksmuseum
(► 22–23), Stedelijk
Museum (► 71)

Audio-tour

Van Gogh's Bedroom at
Arles *(1888)*

*Few artists' life and achievement provoke such
passion as those of Van Gogh (1853–90). See why,
at the world's largest collection of his work.*

This is home to more than 200 Van Gogh paintings, 580
drawings, seven sketchbooks, 750 letters – including the
correspondence with his brother Theo – and Vincent's
Japanese print collection, though not all are on permanent
display. One hundred of the artist's most important works,
displayed chronologically, make it possible to follow his
ten-year artistic odyssey that ended in suicide. Sombre
early works from Holland and Belgium give way to experiments with colour and technique in Paris, swirling colour
and light from Provence, and his anguished work,
Wheatfield With Crows (1890), painted a few days before
he shot himself at the age of 37.

Other canvases on display include *The Potato Eaters*
(1885); *Woman in the Café Le Tambourin* (1887); *The
Yellow House* (1888), depicting the house at Arles Vincent
stayed in with Paul Gaugin; *Sunflowers* (1888); and
Branches With Almond Blossom (1890), sent to Theo on
the birth of his son. You can also see paintings by
Toulouse-Lautrec, Gauguin and other artists from the
period between 1840 and 1920.

Gerrit Rietveld (1888–1964), an exponent of the De Stijl
school of art, designed the museum, which opened in
1973. A dull, concrete exterior hides a bright, glass-roofed
atrium that runs the four-floor building's full height and
floods its exhibition areas with light. Built to accommodate
60,000 visitors a year, the museum now hosts a million.
Temporary exhibitions are mounted in the ellipse-shaped
1999 extension by Japanese architect Kisho Kurokawa.

9
Vondelpark

Cool place on a hot day, the city's green and scented fresh-air store is where Amsterdammers cast off those few inhibitions they have left.

The park retains much of the raffish air it acquired during the 1960s and 1970s, when it was the hippies' Amsterdam *pied à terre*. You can still see the occasional ageing hippie, though nowadays you're more likely to encounter in-line skaters and joggers in Dayglo outfits, along with sunbathers, walkers, cyclists and horse-riders. On a 'quiet' summer walk you're liable to be pelted with frisbees, handballs, footballs, baseballs, basketballs, cricket balls and tennis balls. Assorted performance artists keep things from getting dull – everyone from the Royal Concertgebouw Orchestra to stiltwalkers, taking in mime artists and poets, fire-eaters and jugglers, theatre and dance troupes, rock 'n roll and jazz bands along the way.

Father and son architects J D and L P Zocher laid out and landscaped the park in the 'natural' English style during the 1860s and 1870s. Named after Amsterdam's best-known poet and dramatist, Joost van den Vondel (1587–1679), the park covers 48 hectares with lawns, ornamental lakes, flowers, plants and 120 varieties of tree. Elegant turn-of-the-century town houses and villas border it, and there is both a 19th-century and a 1930s café – neither of which sell the *very* special 'gateau' that goes under the name 'space cake' at unofficial pathside stalls.

➕ 40A1

✉ Between Stadhouderskade and Amstelveenseweg

🕐 Daily dawn–late

🍴 Vertigo (€€, ➤ 97), Het Ronde Blauwe Theehuis (€)

🚌 1, 2, 3, 5, 6, 12, 20

🚤 Museum Boat stop 3

♿ Good

✋ Free

↔ Leidseplein (➤ 20)

❓ Open-air summer festival of concerts and theatre

All dressed up and ready to go for a performance in Vondelpark

10
Westerkerk

The proud Westerkerk tower dominates the Jordaan district

Westerkerk is one of four great churches in the city that symbolise Calvinism's triumph over Catholicism, as well as Amsterdam's Golden Age.

Unlike some historic Amsterdam churches, the grand Dutch Renaissance West Church is still in use for services. Its vast, plainly decorated nave, with wooden barrel vaulting and 12 chandeliers, is Holland's largest. The Hemony organ from 1687 has decorative panels painted by Gerard de Lairesse. Rembrandt and his son Titus are buried here in unknown graves; a memorial to the artist, attached to a pillar in 1906, was copied from a memorial stone visible in *The Night Watch*.

Work on the church began in 1620 under architect Hendrick de Keyser. When he died the following year, his son Pieter took over, and the church opened in 1631. Renovation work between 1985 and 1990 removed centuries of grime, restoring the brick and stone to their original colour.

In summer you can climb the 85m-high Westertoren bell tower that was completed in 1638 – the city's tallest, popularly called 'Lange Jan' (Long John). A spectacular view of the canal-threaded city centre and the Jordaan is your reward. A gold, red and blue Habsburg imperial crown caps the tower, an emblem that in 1489 Maximilian of Austria gave Amsterdam the right to bear on its coat of arms. Listening to the church bells consoled Anne Frank while she hid from the Nazis, and they ring out in an hour-long carillon concert every Tuesday at noon.

The church's coach house, at Prinsengracht 277, is now the Rum Runners Caribbean restaurant (➤ 96); and the house where French philosopher René Descartes lived from 1629 till 1635, while writing his *Treatise on the Passions of the Soul*, is at Westermarkt 6.

✚ 40B4

✉ Prinsengracht 281

☎ 624 7766

🕓 Church: Mon–Sat 11–5, Sun 1–5; tower: Jun–mid-Sep Wed–Sat 10–4

🚌 13, 14, 17, 20

🚢 Museum Boat stop 2

♿ Few

✋ Church free; tower cheap

↔ Anne Frankhuis (➤ 17)

What to See

Above: *say it with tulips – from Amsterdam, naturally*
Right: *traditional costumes are not exactly common in the city, but you can still spot them in nearby villages*

GREATER AMSTERDAM

0   1   2 km

S102

Station
Sloterdijk

N5

Eendrachts-
park

BOS EN LOMMER

Centrale
Markthallen

GEUZENVELD

Erasmuspark

OUD WES

SLOTERMEER

Sloterpark

OVERTOOMSE
VELD

Kostverloren

Sloterplas

Rembrandt-
park

Station
Lelylaan

Van Gogh Muse
Stedelijk Mus

OSDORP

SLOTERVAART

Vondelpark
Concertgebo

NIEUW

Trammuseum
Amsterdam

SLOTEN

Schinkel

Olympisch
Stadion

Ringvaart

RIJKSWEG

A4

A10

Het Nieuwe Meer

Vrije
Universit

NIEUWE
MEER

Bosmuseum

Bosbaan

BUITENVELDE

Grote
Vijver

Het
Amsterdamse
Bos

AMSTELVEE

Luchthaven
Schiphol
(Aviodome)

CoBrA
Museum

A   B   C

Het IJ

S118

NOORD

Flora Park

NIEUWE LEEUWARDERWEG

NIEUWENDAM

A10

SPAARNDAMMERBURT

WH Vliegenbos

SCHELLINGWOUDE

S114

Centraal Station

IJ-TUNNEL

Het IJ

Anne Frankhuis

Beurs van Berlage

Newmetropolis

IJ Haven

Koninklijk Paleis

Oosterdok

Dijksgracht

CENTRUM

Museum het Rembrandthuis

HAVENS OOST

Amsterdams Historisch Museum

Stadhuis en Muziektheater

Natura Artis Magistra (Zoo)

IJ Meer

Rijksmuseum

Nederlandse Bank

OOST

Singelgracht

Muiderpoort Station

Flevo-park

Het Nieuwe Diep

A10

Tropenmuseum en Kindermuseum

Oosterpark

OUD ZUID

Sarphatipark

Amstel

UID

Amstel Kanaal

WATERGRAAFSMEER

Diemer Polder

A2-E231

BERLAGE BRUG

Amstel Station

RAI Congrescentrum

atrixpark

Martin Luther King Park

UTRECHTSE-BRUG

DIEMEN

A10

OVER AMSTEL

A10

Amstel-park

DUIVENDRECHT

Amstel

Duivendrecht

A2-E35

RIJKSWEG

De Rieker

BIJLMERMEER

Amsterdam Arena

Ouderkerker aan-de-Amstel

D

E

F

Amsterdam

Any one of the elements that meld to form Amsterdam's special character would be enough to create a memorable setting. Its thousands of magnificent 17th-century buildings, strung along a web of canals crossed by more than a thousand bridges; its situation below sea-level in a place where, by rights, cold North Sea waves should flow back and forth; the centuries-long tradition of tolerance that made the city a magnet for oppressed minorities long before such a stance became fashionable, or even imaginable, elsewhere; the refusal to settle for what outsiders consider right and proper, but instead to search for solutions to all kinds of social challenges, from prostitution, to drug use and abuse; and how to live harmoniously in a melting pot society. The city's often eccentric lifestyle has a downside, and not everybody takes to its free and easy ways. One thing is sure, though: you'll never be bored.

'Where else in the world are all life's commodities and every conceivable curiosity to be found as easily as here? Where else in the world can one find such absolute freedom?'

RENÉ DESCARTES,
Letter to a friend, 1634

●

Visit the Albert Cuyp street market for bargains and local colour

The streets are paved with orange on Koninginnedag (Queen's Day)

The City of Amsterdam

This city is easy to get to grips with – geographically speaking. Its centre is small enough for locals to think of it as a village, and many sights and attractions lie within easy walking distance of each other. Once you've learned how to work out which way you're facing on the ring canal network, most of your directional problems are over. Should you grow weary of traipsing cobbled streets you can take the weight off your feet aboard a tram, canal boat, water taxi, even a pedalo (water bike).

The top three museums – Rijksmuseum, Van Gogh Museum and Stedelijk Museum – are complemented by a cast of supporting acts covering everything from the city's history, and Holland's glorious maritime past and colonial empire, through theatre and film, to moderately offbeat institutions on such themes as cats and houseboats, and radically offbeat places featuring drugs, torture, tattoos and sex.

There is much more to Amsterdam, however, than history, museums and art. The city's brown cafés, stained by centuries of tobacco smoke, are much-loved institutions that merit the prized Dutch description *'gezellig'* – comfortable, warm, friendly. Nightlife, drinking and dining options are legion, and if you must, you can take yourself to a 'coffee shop' where you can puff your way through as much officially tolerated hashish as you like.

Amsterdam is an attitude as much as a real place. If you already have, or can acquire, the right attitude, you'll find it's a real place, too.

What to See in Amsterdam

ALLARD PIERSON MUSEUM ✪

Amsterdam University houses its archaeological collection in a neo-classical former bank. There are few outstanding objects, but rather bits and pieces from here and there – coins, funerary monuments, mummies, glassware, jewellery, marble, pottery, sculpture and everyday objects. Pharaonic Egypt, Minoan Crete, ancient Greece, Rome and Etruria are reasonably well represented, and there are some good models of pyramids and chariots. Temporary exhibitions are generally more interesting.

THE AMSTEL ✪✪

Amsterdam's river flows south to north into the city, passing some lovely countryside around Ouderkerk aan de Amstel (► 85) before reaching urban reality as it passes under the A10 ring road. The stretch from Utrechtsebrug to the Blauwbrug (Blue Bridge), lined with houseboats, theatres, cafés and riverside homes, presents a busy scene of canal barges, tour boats and private boats

🗺 40C3
✉ Oude Turfmarkt 127
☎ 525 2556
🕐 Tue–Fri 10–5, Sat–Sun and pub hols 1–5. Closed 1 Jan, Easter Sun, 30 Apr, 5 May, Whit Sunday 25 Dec
🚋 4, 9, 14, 16, 20, 24, 25
♿ Good
💰 Moderate

🗺 41E1

travelling up- and downriver. Photographers can't resist the Magere Brug over the Amstel (► 57). As it flows past the Muziektheater and Hôtel de l'Europe, the river gradually loses itself among a maze of city-centre canals.

Tour boats show visitors the sights along the Amstel

AMSTELPARK ✪

This beautiful green area, created in 1972 for a decennial national flower show, the Floriade, lies along the River Amstel on the edge of town. It is hemmed in on the north by the busy A10 ring road and on the west by suburban Buitenveldert. You can stroll around its central pond and through a rosarium and rhododendron garden, get lost in a maze, and visit the Glazenhuis (Glass House) art gallery and a children's farm. De Rieker windmill is outside the park to the south (► 67).

- 🕂 29D1
- ✉ Between Amsteldijk and Europaboulevard
- 🅰 Park: dawn–dusk; Glazenhuis: Mar–Nov Mon–Fri 10–5
- 🍴 Rosarium café-restaurant (€–€€)
- 🚌 Bus 69, 89, 148, 169
- ♿ Very good
- 🎟 Free

AMSTERDAMSE BOS ✪✪✪

It looks natural, but Amsterdam Wood is man-made. Amsterdammers come to this 900-hectare forested park on the city's southern edge for fresh air and to escape from the city. Many bring a picnic when the weather is fine. With its trees and plants firmly established in what was once open polder, the park is home to birds, insects and small animals, and its lakes and wetland zones attract water birds. You can trace its history and learn about the plants and wildlife at the **Bosmuseum**, where a forest diorama goes from day to night at the flick of a switch.

The list of open-air activities is endless. In addition to a bicycle-hire kiosk beside the main entrance, there are stables where you can hire horses and tour the park on bridle-paths, sport facilities, children's play areas, picnic tables, an open-air theatre, a goat farm, and rowing competitions on the 2km-long Roeibaan (rowing lake).

In summer, take a tram ride on an antique car from the Trammuseum at Haarlemmermeerstation (► 72), and on Sundays and holidays, in good weather, a little ferryboat makes trips across the Nieuwe Meer (New Lake).

- 🕂 28B1
- ✉ Main entrance: Amstelveenseweg
- ☎ Visitors Centre and Bosmuseum: 643 1414
- 🅰 Park: always open; Bosmuseum: daily 10–5
- 🍴 De Bosbaan café, De Manegerie café (€–€€)
- 🚌 Bus 170, 171, 172
- ♿ Very good
- 🎟 Free

Along the Amstel

Cycling is a key ingredient in the Amsterdam experience and on this riverside route you get a breath of fresh country air as a bonus. Pause at the start for a look at the Blauwbrug (Blue Bridge).

Facing south (upriver), cycle along the Amstel's right bank (the river should be on your right), across Nieuwe Herengracht and Nieuwe Keizersgracht to the Magere Brug (➤ 57). Cross Nieuwe Prinsengracht to a set of locks beside which stands the Koninklijke Theater Carré (➤ 112). Continue over Sarphatistraat to the Amstel Inter Continental Hotel.

The city's top hotel, the Amstel is favoured by blue bloods, Hollywood superstars and top musicians.

Dogleg around behind the hotel, back to the river on Weesperzijde, and past De IJsbreker contemporary music theatre. Continue to the Berlagebrug, where you cross to the left bank.

The bridge, which has red-and-black painted lampposts, was built in 1932 by Hendrik Petrus Berlage, designer of the Beurs van Berlage (➤ 38), and a forerunner of the Amsterdam School of Architecture.

Continue south, past Martin Luther Kingpark and houseboats moored along Amsteldijk, to Amstelpark (➤ 33), the De Rieker windmill (➤ 67) and a statue of Rembrandt.

You are now in open countryside, passing through idyllic riverside scenery on the way to Ouderkerk aan de Amstel (➤ 85). Explore the pretty, historic village.

For the return to Amsterdam, take Ouderkerkerdijk on the right bank of the river.

You pass through several hamlets on this tranquil road.

Keep going to busy Utrechtsebrug. Cross over to Amsteldijk and stay on the left bank all the way back to the Blue Bridge.

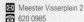

Carré: theatrical highlight down by the riverside

Distance
20km

Time
4–6 hours

Start/end point
Blauwbrug
🚏 41D2
Ⓜ Waterlooplein
🚊 9, 14, 20

Lunch
't Klein Kalfje (€, ➤ 94)

Bike hire
MacBike
✉ Meester Visserplein 2
☎ 620 0985

AMSTERDAMS HISTORISCH MUSEUM (► 16, TOP TEN)

AMSTERDAMS VERZETSMUSEUM ✪

The Resistance Museum tells the story of Amsterdam's five years (1940–5) under Nazi occupation during World War II. Among the events it highlights are the 1941 February Strike against the deportation of the city's Jewish population, and the terrible 'Hunger Winter' of 1944–5, as well as the minutiae of underground activities: illegal newspapers, espionage, sabotage, assassination.

✚ 41E3
✉ Plantage Kerklaan 61a
☎ 620 2535
🕐 Tue–Fri 10–5, Sat–Mon & public hols 12–5. Closed 1 Jan, 30 Apr, 25 Dec
🚊 6, 9, 14, 20
♿ Good
🎟 Cheap

ANNE FRANKHUIS (► 17, TOP TEN)

ARTIS ✪✪✪

Holland's largest zoo houses more than 6,000 animals, including lions, tigers, leopards, elephants and rhinoceroses. Its full name is Natura Artis Magistra: 'Nature, Teacher of the Arts', and among its attractions are extensive gardens whose range of tree and plant varieties almost rivals that of nearby Hortus Botanicus (► 49). Artis does its best to replicate the animals' natural environment, using glass and perspex to get you close to them. Good examples are the Reptile House, with its steamy jungle settings, and the renovated 1882 Aquarium, which has glass tanks in which seals disport, as well as displays on coral reefs, the Amazon and a surprising, cut-away view of an Amsterdam canal, with fish swimming beside a sunken bicycle and other urban detritus. To get value from the steep admission price, visit, at no extra charge, the excellent Planetarium, Geological Museum and Zoological Museum. If you have children don't let them miss the children's farm.

✚ 41E2
✉ Plantage Kerklaan 38–40
☎ 523 3400
🕐 Daily 9–5 (to 6 Apr–Oct); Planetarium closed Mon morning
🍴 Artis restaurant (€)
🚊 9, 14, 20
⛴ Artis Express boat from Centraal Station; Museum Boat stop 5
♿ Good
🎟 Very expensive

Above: Artis has a way with animals, and a leafy, garden-like setting

In the Know

If you only have a short time to visit Amsterdam and would like to get a real flavour of the city, here are some ideas:

10
Ways to be a Local

Go Dutch. Almost everyone speaks English, but an occasional *Alstublieft* (please) and *Dank u wel* (thank you) can go a long way.

Don't walk in bicycle lanes. And don't complain if a cyclist thumps you because you did.

Don't be seen dead on a water bike – by all means be seen alive on one,

Waterborne revellers celebrate Queen's Day (30 April)

though, for a great experience that many locals pass up.

Take flowers (tulips are OK) if someone invites you

Settling into Café 't Smalle's welcoming ambience

to their home for dinner.

Head for a café terrace at the first hint of sunshine.

Eat raw herring at a street stall.

Wear something orange on Koninginnedag, Queen Beatrix's official birthday (30 April).

Don't criticise Holland, the Dutch way of doing things or the Queen; it's OK to make jibes about provincials and other members of the royal family.

Get the time right. If you have an appointment at 30 minutes past the hour, half ten say, make sure it's not *half tien*, which means 9:30, not 10:30.

Absorb the atmosphere in a 'coffee shop'. Few Amsterdammers actually do smoke joints in these, in fact, though they can if they want to.

Join the crowds in search of a bargain, or just browsing, at the Albert Cuyp street market

10
Top Places to Have Lunch

Café Américain (► 93)
Café Roux (► 93)
De Jaren (► 94)
Excelsior (€€€)
✉ Hôtel de l'Europe, Nieuwe Doelenstraat 2–8 ☎ 531 1777. Formal elegance and top-flight continental cuisine.
't Klein Kalfje (► 94)
De Kas (► 94)
Luxembourg (► 95)
Pancake Bakery (€)
✉ Prinsengracht 191 ☎ 625 1333. Traditional and wildly inventive pancakes.
Royal Café De Kroon (► 96)
Vertigo (► 97)

10
Top Activities

Pass an hour in the 'company' of Anne Frank, in the secret refuge where she wrote her famous diary (► 17).
Visit Zandvoort on Sunday, whatever the weather, and walk up and down along the beach (► 89).
Hire a bicycle (► 34) and dice with the trams

at Leidseplein.
Spend an evening in a traditional Amsterdam brown café (► this page and ► 114).
Take a tour by canal boat; it's the best way to get a quick overview of the city (► 67).
Hear the Royal Concertgebouw Orchestra at the Concertgebouw (► 44).
Applaud Amsterdam's ace football team Ajax at Amsterdam ArenA (► 115).
Spend a few hours at the Albert Cuypmarkt and Waterlooplein flea market, or wander around one of the other markets listed (► 106).

Roam the city on a bike – the locals do

Eat your way through the 10–20 little dishes of a *rijsttafel*, an Indonesian speciality.
Beg, borrow, steal, or even buy ice-skates if the canals freeze (► 115).

5
Best Views From

• Herengracht bridge at Thorbeckeplein (► 47).
• IJ Ferry (► 50).
• Magere Brug (► 57).
• Westerkerk tower (► 26).
• Zuiderkerk tower (► 75).

10
Best Brown Cafés

► 114
• De Druif
• De Engelbewaarder
• Hoppe
• De Karpershoek
• 't Loosje
• Papeneiland
• De Reiger
• Reijnders
• 't Smalle
• Tabac

ATHENAEUM ILLUSTRE ✪

An elaborate Renaissance gateway from 1571 marks the entrance to Amsterdam's first university. Founded in 1631 and established here the following year, it took over the 15th-century Gothic Agnietenkapel (St Agnes Chapel) and Franciscan convent, which was used as an arsenal by the Dutch navy after the 1578 religious *Alteratie*. It now houses the Universiteitsmuseum (University Museum), embracing the university's history, famous professors and students.

🚩 40C3
✉ Oudezijds Voorburgwal 231
☎ 525 3339
🕐 Mon–Fri 9–5, Sun (late Jun to mid-Nov) 2–5. Closed pub hols
🚌 4, 9, 14, 16, 20, 24, 25
🎫 Free (except special exhibitions)

AVIODOME ✪✪

The National Aviation Museum, housed in a geodesic dome at Schiphol Airport, has aircraft and models of aircraft from 1903 onwards. Some are parked outside, some have mannequin ground crews and passengers, others hang from the ceiling. They include the world's first commercial airliner, a Fokker F7a in 1920s KLM livery; a World War I Fokker DR-1 triplane fighter; a World War II Spitfire; and a former Royal Netherlands Air Force Starfighter interceptor.

🚩 28A1
✉ Westelijke Randweg 201, Schiphol
☎ 406 8000
🕐 Apr–Sep daily 10–5; Oct–Mar Tue–Fri 10–5, Sat–Sun, pub hols 12–5. Closed Mon (except school and pub hols). Closed 1 Jan, 25 & 31 Dec
🚉 Schiphol 🚻 Good
🎫 Moderate

BEGIJNHOF (► 18, TOP TEN)

BEURS VAN BERLAGE ✪✪

Hendrik Petrus Berlage's 1903, red-brick Beurs (Stock Exchange) is an early work of the Amsterdam School, whose members made a dramatic break with 19th-century architecture. No longer the stock exchange, it hosts concerts and exhibitions, and its south wing is home to the Beurs van Berlage Museum, with displays on the Stock Exchange's history and temporary exhibitions on varying themes. The interior has interesting glass and wrought-iron decoration and murals. Among exterior sculptures, a relief of two fishermen and a sick dog in a boat illustrates a legend of the city's foundation (► 44). Climb the clock tower for a view of the old centre. Trees and 19th-century wrought-iron street lamps dot neighbouring Beursplein.

🚩 41D4
✉ Damrak 277
☎ 624 0141
🕐 Tue–Fri 10–4
🍴 Café Rainieri (€)
🚌 4, 9, 14, 16, 20, 24, 25
🚻 Good
🎫 Moderate

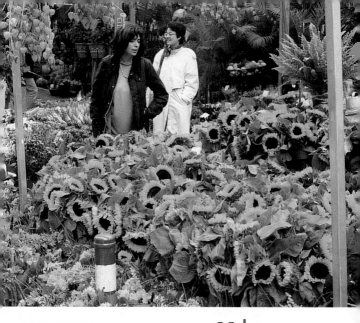

BIJBELS MUSEUM ✪✪

The Biblical Museum's twin canal houses, with richly decorated neck-gables and a courtyard with an ornamental garden, are worth visiting for their intrinsic interest. They were built in 1662 by architect Philips Vingboons for wealthy merchant Jacob Cromhout. In 1717, Jacob de Wit painted the main hall's ceiling with classical scenes. The collection focuses on life in the Holy Land during biblical times and on Judaism and Christianity through the centuries. Objects on view include a model of ancient Jerusalem, models of the temples of Solomon and Herod, one of them dating from 1730, and a model of the Tabernacle from 1851, archaeological finds and paintings of biblical scenes. Bibles include the first one printed in the Low Countries, in 1477, and a first edition of the authorised Dutch translation from 1637.

BLOEMENMARKT ✪✪

Like an Impressionist artist's palette fallen from the sky and drifting along the canal, the Singel Flower Market, Amsterdam's only remaining floating market, is a riot of colour. There has been a floating market here since the 17th century; now a row of 15 shops on permanently moored barges sell bunches of freshly cut flowers as fast as the sales staff can wrap them, along with plants, packets of tulip bulbs with phytosanitary certificates that allows their import into many countries, and all kinds of green-fingered accessories. Buying flowers along the fragrantly scented canalside is an Amsterdam ritual, though prices are no cheaper than those in shops. Tulips are especially popular.

🞢 40B3
✉ Herengracht 366–368
☎ 624 2436
🕐 Mon–Sat 10–5, Sun and pub hols 1–5. Closed 1 Jan, 30 Apr
🚌 1, 2, 5
🚤 Museum Boat stop 4
♿ None 🞖 Moderate

Above: *there's no better place to buy flowers than the floating Flower Market*

🞢 40C2
✉ Singel (between Muntplein and Koningsplein)
🕐 Mon–Sat 9:30–5:30 (till 5 Sat).
🚌 1, 2, 4, 5, 9, 14, 16, 20, 24, 25
🚤 Museum Boat stop 4
♿ Good
🞖 Free

CENTRAL AMSTERDAM

Het IJ

BUIKSLOTERWEG

Noord Hollandsch Kanaal

MEEUWENLAAN

DE RUIJTERKADE

IJ-TUNNEL

KNSM Eiland

Centraal Station

STATIONS PLEIN Ⓜ Centraal Station

IJ-Haven

ⓘ

ex & St Nicolaaskerk
orture
useums ● Schreierstoren

PIET HEINKADE

Museum Amstelring

Scheepvarthuis

Dijksgracht

Oosterdok

PRINS HENDRIKKADE

Newmetropolis

ude
erk

Erotisch
Museum

Waag

KATTENBURGERSTRAAT

Tattoo NIEUWMARKT
Museum
Hasj
Marihuana Ⓜ
Hemp Museum
Oostindisch Huis
Trippenhuis
Zuiderkerk

Nieuw-
Markt

Montelbaan-
storen

Nederlands
Scheepvaart Museum

Katenburgervaart

Wittenburgervaart

Museum het
Rembrandthuis

Amsterdams
Verzetsmuseum

Nieuwe Vaart

Holland
Experience
Stadhuis en
Muziektheater

Mozes en Aäronkerk

MR VISSER
PLEIN
WATERLOO
PLEIN

Wertheim
Park

Portugese
Synagoge

Entrepotdok

Werf 't
Kromhout

Planetarium

De Gooier

Waterlooplein Ⓜ
AMSTELSTR BLAUW
BRUG

Hortus
Botanicus
Plantage

Hollandse
Schouwburg

Natura Artis
Magistra
(Zoo)

Joods
Historisch
Museum

Keizersgracht

Zoölogisch
Museum-
Aquarium

Willet-
Holthuysen

NIEUWE KERKSTRAAT

MIDDENLAAN

MAGERE
BRUG

Nieuwe Prinsengracht

SARPHATISTRAAT

Singelgracht

Weesper-
plein Ⓜ

Koninklijke
Theater
Carré

SARPHATISTRAAT

MAURITSKADE

Tropenmuseum
en Kindermuseum

Oosterpark

FREDERIKS-
PLEIN

RHIJNSPOORPLEIN

Nederlandse
Bank

De Ijsbreker

Gasthuis

OOSTERPARKSTRAAT

STADHOUDERSKADE

Sarphatipark CEINTURBAAN

Amstel

Wibautstraat Ⓜ

0   200   400 m

D   E   F

41

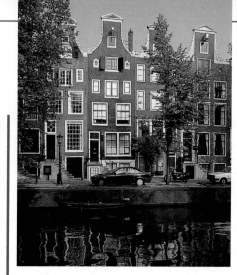

Converted 17th-century warehouses mirrored in the Brouwersgracht

 40B5
✉ Between Lijnbaansgracht and Singel
🍴 De Belhamel (▶ 92); Café Tabac, Brouwersgracht 101 (€)
🚊 1, 2, 5, 13, 17, 20

BROUWERSGRACHT ⭐⭐

The 'Brewers' Canal' owes its name to 16th- and 17th-century brewery *pakhuizen* (warehouses), many now chic apartments. Attractively restored, De Kroon (The Crown) at No 118, and the modern Blauwe Burgt apartment block show how old and new are trying to live in harmony. The point where Brouwersgracht joins Prinsengracht is one of the most photogenic spots in the city. At Herenmarkt, off Brouwersgracht, is West-Indisch Huis (West India House), which in 1623 became the Dutch West India Company's headquarters. In its courtyard is a bronze statue of Peter Stuyvesant, governor of Nieuw Amsterdam from 1646 until 1664, when the British took over and renamed it New York. A sculpture depicts the first Dutch settlement on Manhattan Island, founded in 1624.

✉ Rijksmuseum, Leidseplein, Keizersgracht/ Leidsestraat (rarely open), Anne Frankhuis
📞 626 5574
🕐 Apr–Jun and Sep–Oct daily 10–6; Jul–Aug daily 10–10 (may close earlier)
♿ None
💷 Expensive

CANAL BIKE ⭐⭐

Amsterdammers scorn them, but it's hard to think of a better way of touring the city's canals, short of having your own boat. On these two- and four-seat pedalos (water bikes) you can view the canals and their gabled houses at your own pace and from a unique perspective. You can hire a pedalo at one of four Canal Bike moorings near popular sights around the centre and leave it at another. The company provides maps and basic 'rules of the road'.

 41D4
✉ Stationsplein
🍴 1e Klas (€–€€), Smits Koffiehuis (€)
🚊 1, 2, 4, 5, 9, 13, 16, 17, 20, 24, 25
🚢 Museum Boat stop 1
♿ Excellent

CENTRAAL STATION ⭐⭐

Amsterdam's main railway station is a bustling hub that captures the city's energy, bundles it up and sends it hurrying off again in all directions. Eleven of 17 tram lines converge here, along with four metro lines, two passenger ferries, any number of buses, canal buses, taxis, watertaxis and tour boats (including the Museumboat and the Canal Bus). There are two VVV (Vereniging voor

Vreemdelingenverkeer) tourist offices, one inside on platform one, the other outside on Stationsplein; a Grenswisselkantoor (GWK) exchange office; cafés; shops; buskers; barrel-organs; a million bicycles, commuters, tourists, backpackers, pickpockets and junkies.

Petrus Josephus Hubertus Cuypers designed this work of architectural note, which opened in 1889 on three artificial islands in the IJ channel. Cuypers, who also designed the Rijksmuseum (► 22–3), repeated his earlier trick of mixing Dutch Renaissance elements with his own neo-gothic inclinations, to produce a twin-towered temple of transport that, at the time, many Amsterdammers were inclined to hate.

CLAES CLAESZOON HOFJE ✪

Wealthy cloth merchant Claes Claeszoon Anslo founded this almshouse in 1615. It is really two *hofjes*, whose tiny houses surrounding two picturesque little courtyards are now music students' homes. You can visit the courtyards when the outer door is open.

🚹 40B4
✉ Egelantiersstraat 18–50/ Eerste Egelantiersdwars-straat 1–3
🚊 13, 14, 17, 20
💲 Free

COBRA MUSEUM ✪✪

Begun in 1948, the Cobra group took its name from the founding artists' home cities: Copenhagen, Brussels, Amsterdam. In creating a new, post-war art, they reached for childlike, spontaneous imagery, often done in bold colours with crayon, that laid the foundations of abstract expressionism. Their first exhibition, at Amsterdam's Stedelijk Museum (► 71) in 1949, ignited fierce contro-versy. Cobra has since become more accepted and now has a permanent home. Vividly expressionistic works by Karel Appel, Asger Jorn and Pierre Alechinsky are among those on display at this dazzlingly white museum in respectable, suburban Amstelveen.

🚹 28C1
✉ Sandbergplein 1–3, Amstelveen
☎ 547 5050
🕐 Tue–Sun 11–5. Closed 1 Jan, 1 Apr, 30 Apr, 25 Dec
🍴 Café-restaurant (€)
🚊 51, Amstelveen
🚌 5
♿ Excellent
💲 Moderate

Concertgebouw strikes just the right notes for classical music

 40B1
 Concertgebouwplein 2–6
☎ 671 8345
🕐 Box office daily 10–7
🍴 Café (€)
🚋 3, 5, 12, 16, 20
Museum Boat stop 3
⚫ Good
👆 Lunchtime concerts free; otherwise moderate to expensive
❓ Guided tours by prior arrangement Sun 9:30

CONCERTGEBOUW

Classical musicians consider the home of the Koninklijke Concertgebouworkest (Royal Concertgebouw Orchestra), opened in 1888, to be one of the world's three most accoustically perfect concert halls. Architect Adolf van Gendt designed it in neo-Dutch renaissance style with a neo-classical colonnade. Portrait busts of Beethoven, Sweelinck and Bach greet you at the entrance, and a sculpted lyre adorns the roof. There are two performance halls, the Grote Zaal (Grand Hall) and the Kleine Zaal (Little Hall), which is used for recitals. Refurbishment during the 1980s included adding a new wing, at the cost of spoiling the building's original lines.

🚩 40B1
 Paulus Potterstraat 2–6
☎ 305 5555
🕐 Daily 9–5. Closed 25 Dec
🚋 1, 2, 10, 16
Museum Boat stop 3
⚫ Few
👆 Free

COSTER DIAMONDS

Coster Diamonds is one of the quality diamond workshops in the city to offer guided tours. Amsterdam got into the diamond business around 1586, when diamond-workers and traders from Bruges and Antwerp, many of whom were Jewish, fled to the city to escape the Spanish Inquisition. Such famous diamonds as the Cullinan and Koh-I-Noor were cut in Amsterdam. The Jewish community played a prominent role in the industry until World War II, when many Jewish workers perished in Nazi concentration camps. Coster's 30-minute tour includes a brief history of diamonds, and it is fascinating to watch the company's craftspeople at work, cutting, polishing, sorting and setting.

DID YOU KNOW?

A shaggy dog story competes with the historical record of Amsterdam's foundation. Two fishermen and a dog, their boat caught in a Zuiderzee storm, made landfall at what is now Zeedijk. The dog jumped on to dry land and promptly threw up, thereby marking the spot. An image of two men and a seasick dog in a boat appears on the city's old coat of arms, which you can see at various places around town.

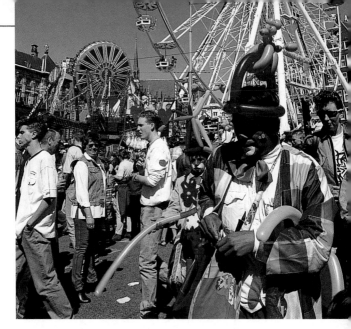

DAM ❤❤❤

Foreigners say 'Dam Square', but to Amsterdammers it's 'the Dam', though it is evidently a square and not a dam. The original dam, built in the mid-13th century, protected what was then a fishing village. As Amsterdam expanded, flood defences were built further away and the Dam developed into the political, commercial, monumental and ceremonial heart of the city, containing the Royal Palace (► 19), Nieuwe Kerk (► 62) and Nationaal Monument (► 60). It frequently hosts fairs, open-air concerts, exhibitions, shows and various other events, and is where the important tourist business of feeding the pigeons is done.

➕ 40C3
🚋 1, 2, 4, 5, 9, 13, 14, 16, 17, 20, 24, 25

Above: *anything can happen, and often does, in the city's monumental square – the Dam*

DE EILANDEN (THE ISLANDS) ❤

Along the IJ waterfront's southern shore, redevelopment is transforming artificial islands that once held harbour installations, boat repair yards and warehouses. On the Western Islands of Prinseneiland, Bickerseiland and Realeneiland, northwest of Centraal Station, old warehouses are now desirable apartments. On KNSM Eiland, east of Centraal Station, modern apartments replace cargo-handling facilities.

➕ 40B5
✉ IJ waterfront
🚋 3; bus 18, 22, 32, 35, 39, 59

EROTISCH MUSEUM ❤

'The Art of Erotics' is how the owners subtitle their establishment. Prints and drawings, including some by John Lennon, and photographs aim to uncover the artistic side of eroticism and sado-masochism. Attractions include a maquette of a Red Light District scene and an adult cartoon version of *Snow White and the Seven Dwarfs*.

➕ 41D4
✉ Oudezijds Achterburgwal 54
☎ 624 7303
🕐 Mon–Thu, Sun 11AM–1AM; Fri–Sat 11AM–2AM
🚋 4, 9, 14, 16, 20, 24, 25
♿ Few Cheap

45

⊞ 41F2
✉ Funenkade 7
☎ 622 8325
🕐 Wed–Sun 3–8
🚃 7, 10
♿ Good 🎫 Free

⊞ 40C4
✉ Oudezijds Achterburgwal 148
☎ 623 5961
🕐 Daily 11AM–10PM
🚃 4, 9, 14, 16, 20, 24, 25
♿ Few
🎫 Very expensive

Below: *beer on the hoof from Heineken's promotion team*

⊞ 40C1
✉ Stadhouderskade 78
☎ 523 9666
🕐 Guided tours (1½ hours; over-18s only) Tue–Sun 10–6. Closed 1 Jan, 25 Dec
🍴 Heineken Bar
🚃 16, 24, 25
🚤 Museum Boat stop 3
♿ Few (call ahead)
🎫 Expensive

DE GOOIER (FUNENMOLEN) ✪

Built in 1725 on a brick base with octagonal body and thatched wooden frame, one of few surviving city windmills houses Brouwerij 't IJ, a small brewery and *proeflokaal* (➤ 114). Occasionally whirls into action.

HASJ MARIHUANA HEMP MUSEUM ✪

An 'educational' tour informs you of the good things that ostensibly flow from smoking and otherwise assimilating hemp's multifarious, stimulating by-products. You will see displays on historical, medicinal, religious, recreational and practical uses of hashish and marijuana.

DID YOU KNOW?

Contrary to popular opinion, drugs are not legal in Holland. Penalties for possessing and selling heroin, cocaine and other 'hard' drugs are heavy. 'Soft' drugs, such as hashish and marijuana, are also illegal, but Amsterdam's authorities tolerate their sale in small quantities in licensed 'coffee shops'. You are allowed to possess up to 30g of these drugs for personal use, though coffee shops can sell you only 5g at a time.

HEINEKEN EXPERIENCE AMSTERDAM ✪✪

The old Heineken brewery from 1868 hung up its mash-staff in 1988 and reopened two years later as a museum. Its exhibition 'galleries' include former fermentation tanks that once held a million glassfuls of beer and now host a multiscreen video show that sums up 5,000 years of beery history in five minutes. You can tour the brewing facilities, visit stables where Heineken keeps its promotion team's antique drays and the horses to pull them, and finish by sampling the golden brew itself.

HERENGRACHT   ✪✪✪

No fewer than 400 buildings along this historic 2.3km canal are protected monuments. Just as self-made gentlemen were more highly regarded in 17th-century Holland than emperors and princes, so the Gentlemen's Canal, begun in 1609, was a better address than the contemporaneous Keizersgracht and Prinsengracht. The higher you progress in house numbers, the more ostentatious become the gabled canalside mansions, until you reach the apex of social exclusivity, the Golden Bend, between Leidsestraat and Vijzelstraat.

Highlights of Herengracht's horseshoe-shaped course through the city are its oldest warehouses at Nos 43–5, from around 1600; Theater Insititut Nederlands at Nos 168–72 (➤ 72); Bijbels Museum at No 366 (➤ 39); matching neck-gabled houses, the 'twin sisters', at Nos 390–2 and 'twin brothers' at Nos 409–11; the Jewel of Canal Houses at No 475; Kattenkabinet (Cat Museum) at No 497; the mayoral residence at No 502; and Museum Willet-Holthuysen at No 605 (➤ 59).

HOLLAND EXPERIENCE   ✪✪

Sit in an aeroplane seat, strap yourself in, metaphorically speaking, and head off on a tour of Holland's landscapes and attractions, by way of a multidimensional film show accompanied by movement, sights, sounds and smells. Tulip fields, skating on frozen canals, Rembrandt's *The Night Watch*, 80,000 litres of water gushing towards you in a simulated dike collapse, Queen Beatrix – it's all here. There are also static exhibitions on farming and fishing; even the toilets take you on a 'trip' through the Dutch landscape!

🕂 40C4
🍴 Bars, cafés and restaurants (€–€€€)
🚊 1, 2, 4, 5, 13, 14, 16, 17, 20, 24, 25
🚢 Museum Boat stop 4

Above: *elegant merchants' houses line Herengracht's prestigious banks*

🕂 41D3
✉ Waterlooplein 17
☎ 422 2233
🕐 Daily 10–6:15 (shows at 10:30, 11, 12, 1, 2, 3, 4, 5, and 5:30)
🚇 Waterlooplein
🚊 9, 14, 20
🚢 Museum Boat stop 5
♿ Very good
💲 Expensive

The Canal Ring

This stroll along the *grachtengordel* takes you through the heart of Golden Age Amsterdam.

From its junction with the Amstel, walk along Herengracht, keeping the canal on your left–hand side, to Museum Willet-Holthuysen (➤ 59) then to Thorbeckeplein. Cross the canal and go south along Reguliersgracht to Keizersgracht. Turn right along the canal to Museum Van Loon (➤ 59).

Tour the museum, one of the city's finest canal houses.

Turn right on Vijzelstraat then left on Herengracht.

The next canal bend is the famous Golden Bend, where the city's richest 17th-century citizens had their homes.

Keep going along Herengracht, across Leidse-straat, to the Bijbels Museum (➤ 39). Turn left on Huidenstraat and right on Keizersgracht.

Note the neo-classical Felix Meritis (Happiness from Merit) building dating from 1787 at No 324, former headquarters of a Calvinist scientific and philosophical society.

Keep going on Keizersgracht, turn left on Reestraat, and right on Prinsengracht. Cross Raadhuisstraat to Westermarkt.

Visit the Westerkerk (➤ 26) and see the Homomonument, a pink granite monument dedicated to all gay and lesbian people persecuted for their sexual orientation, and a statue of Anne Frank. Visit the Anne Frankhuis (➤ 17).

Turn right on Leliegracht, and right on Herengracht to the Theatermuseum (➤ 72). Turn around and go north on Herengracht, turn left on Herenstraat, cross Keizersgracht, and right on Prinsengracht to Noordermarkt.

Visit the Noorderkerk (➤ 63).

Take Prinsengracht to Brouwersgracht.

Golden Age houses along Herengracht

Distance
14km

Time
4 hours, longer if you visit museums, churches and markets along the way

Start point
Southern end of Herengracht at junction with the River Amstel
➕ 40C2
🚇 Waterlooplein
🚋 4, 9, 14, 20
🚤 Museum Boat stop 5

End point
Brouwersgracht
➕ 40B5
🚇 Centraal Station
🚋 1, 2, 4, 5, 9, 13, 16, 17, 20, 24, 25 (from Centraal Station)
🚤 Museum Boat stop 1

Lunch
Het Land van Walem (➤ 94)
Luxembourg (➤ 95)

HOLLANDSCHE SCHOUWBURG

Only the ruined façade remains of this operetta theatre from 1892, which in 1941 became the Jewish-only Joodsche Schouwburg, an assembly point for Dutch Jews awaiting deportation to concentration camps. It is now a memorial to those 'who ... did not return', with a list of deportees' family names, an eternal flame and a small museum showing items belonging to some of the 60,000 people the Nazis herded here on their way to death.

🔲 41E2
✉ Plantage Middenlaan 24
☎ 626 9945
🕐 Daily 11–4
🚌 6, 9, 14, 20
♿ Very good
✋ Free

HORTUS BOTANICUS

With 250,000 flowers and 115,000 plants and trees from more than 8,000 varieties, including rare and endangered species, the city's botanical garden has one of the world's largest collections. Founded in 1638 as the Hortus Medicus, for growing medicinal plants and herbs from the Dutch East and West Indies, Australia, South Africa and Japan, Holland's second oldest such garden, after Leiden's (1587), moved here in 1682. At the turn of the century it expanded as a botanical research centre attached to Amsterdam University, and in 1987, when this role ended, went independent and has flourished ever since. This colourful, scented oasis is a great place to escape the crowds. Highlights include the Semicircle, a replica of part of its 1682 layout; the Tri-Climate House, opened in 1993, that brings together African, South American and Mediterranean plants; the Palm House, with 300-year-old palm trees that are among the world's oldest; and the Mexico/California Desert House.

🔲 41D2
✉ Plantage Middenlaan 2a
☎ 625 9021
🕐 Apr–Oct, Mon–Fri 9–5,
   Sat–Sun 11–5; Nov–Mar,
   Mon–Fri 9–4, Sat–Sun
   11–4. Closed 1 Jan,
   25 Dec
🍴 De Oranjerie (€)
🚌 9, 14, 20
🚢 Museum Boat stop 5
♿ Very good
✋ Moderate

Above: *rainforest below sea level at Hortus Botanicus*

49

Above: *passing through the Sint-Antoniessluis in the Jewish Quarter*

HET IJ   ✪✪

The IJ (pronounced like 'eye' in English), an inlet of the IJsselmeer lake, was once the city's harbour. In the 17th century, warehouses filled with exotic products brought by Dutch merchant ships from all over the world lined the waterfront. Although large cargo ships now use newer facilities in the Westport, beside the North Sea Canal, the IJ remains busy with canal barges, pleasure craft, tour boats and an occasional warship and cruise liner. Free passenger-and-bicycle ferries shuttle back and forth across the channel between the rear of Centraal Station and Amsterdam Noord, affording a fine view of the harbour during their brief crossings. On Sundays and public holidays (excluding Koninginnedag, 30 April) from Easter until mid-October, a Historic Ferry tour leaves from the dock behind Centraal Station for two-hour cruises around the old harbour installations in the eastern IJ.

For an insight into the IJ's colourful maritime past, visit the Nederlands Scheepvaartmuseum (➤ 60) and the redeveloped Western and Eastern Islands.

JODENHOEK   ✪✪

Jewish refugees escaping persecution in Europe began arriving in Amsterdam in the 16th century, settling on cheap, marshy land between Nieuwmarkt and the Amstel, around what is now Waterlooplein and Jodenbreestraat. Little remains of the once thriving Jewish Quarter, which, until World War II, never descended to the status of a ghetto. Of the city's 60,000-strong pre-war Jewish population, only about 6,000 survived the Holocaust. During the 1944–5 Hunger Winter, Amsterdammers stripped wood from the quarter's empty buildings to burn as fuel and many unsafe houses were demolished after the war, with more falling victim to redevelopment. Remnants and echoes include the Joods Historisch Museum (see below), the Hollandsche Schouwburg (➤ 49), the 1675 Portugees-Israëlietische Synagoge (➤ 65), Waterlooplein Flea Market (➤ 106), and a Waterlooplein monument to Jewish Resistance fighters.

A silver menorah inside the Jewish Museum

JOODS HISTORISCH MUSEUM ❂❂❂

The remarkable Jewish Historical Museum, occupying four former synagogues in the heart of the Jewish Quarter (see above), records four centuries of Jewish history, identity, religion and culture in the Netherlands. Glassed-in walkways connect the Ashkenazi Synagogue (1670) to the Obbene (1686), Dritt (1700) and New (1752) synagogues. Opened in 1987, the museum puts on temporary exhibitions on international Jewish themes in addition to displaying its permanent collection, which includes historical paintings, decorations, religious and ceremonial objects, clothing, a section on the Holocaust and contemporary Jewish art.

In the square behind the museum is a sculpture called *The Dockworker*, commemorating the February 1941 general strike, led by the city's dockworkers, against Nazi deportation of the Jewish population.

➕ 41D2
✉ Jonas Daniël Meijerplein 2–4
☎ 626 9945
🕐 Daily 11–5. Closed Yom Kippur
🍴 Kosher café (€)
Ⓜ Waterlooplein
🚊 9, 14, 20
� Museum Boat stop 5
♿ Very good
✋ Moderate

DID YOU KNOW?

In what must have been music to Jewish ears, the great Dutch jurist and humanist Hugo Grotius (1583–1645), in his *Remonstratie* (1614), welcomed Jewish refugees who had fled to Holland to escape persecution: 'Plainly God desires them to live somewhere. Why not here rather than elsewhere? The scholars among them may even be of service to us by teaching us the Hebrew language.'

Food & Drink

Gone are the days when Amsterdam was known for its stodgy, unimaginative Dutch food. The scene has been transformed by an influx of cuisine styles from around the world.

Above: *Dutch bakers sell a range of tasty koeken (cakes)*
Below: *Gouda cheese*

Borrelhapjes
For taking the edge off your *jenever* and *pils*, two popular 'drink snacks' are *bitterballen* (bitter balls), deep-fried balls of vegetable paste; and *vlammetjes* (little flames), mini spring rolls filled with meat and *sambal*, a hot Indonesian spice.

Breakfast
A Dutch breakfast (*ontbijt*) usually comprises coffee, tea or hot chocolate, a boiled egg, slices of cheese, ham and salami, bread, gingerbread, butter and jam.

Lunch
You can eat a dinner-type meal in a restaurant, but Amsterdammers prefer a light lunch, often bought from a neighbourhood fish stall. This could be *maatjes* (► Seafood) or *lekkerbek* (fried fish). In an *eetcafé* (bar-restaurant), a traditional favourite is *uitsmijter* ('bouncer'), consisting of fried eggs and ham on bread.

Traditional
In the past, people needed substantial food to combat a climate that delivers lots of rain and wind. Traditional dishes include *erwtensoep* (ultra-thick pea and ham soup); *stamppot* (mashed vegetables with sausage); *hutspot* (beef stew); *boerenkool met worst* (kale with sausage); and *pannekoeken* (pancakes) with toppings that range from bacon and cheese to *stroop* (syrup) and sugar. *Patat* (french fries) are served with mayonnaise (*fritessaus*).

Seafood

Maatjes (raw herring) is a genuine Dutch treat, bought from street stalls, served with raw onion, and eaten whole or chopped into slices. Almost as popular is *gerookte paling* (smoked eel), traditionally from the IJsselmeer. In months with an 'r' in them, you can eat *mosselen* (mussels) and *oesters* (oysters) from the pure waters of Zeeland's Eastern Scheldt estuary. Grey North Sea prawns are popular and tasty. All kinds of other fish are available, including cod, sole, plaice, turbot, salmon and halibut, as well as Mediterranean and tropical species.

Indonesian

The Dutch East Indies were the jewel of Holland's colonial empire. In a reversal of fortunes, Indonesian cuisine has conquered the former mother country. Highlight of the menu is

Indonesian food is popular and widely available in the city

rijsttafel (rice table), a cascade of up to 20 or more dishes ranging from mild to volcanically spicy. *Rijsttafel* was invented by the colonial Dutch, and there is a tendency to look down on it as being for tourists only, yet it provides a good introduction to Indonesian cuisine. As menus often have no English translation, look for such items as *ayam* (chicken), *ikan* (fish), *telor* (egg), *rendang* (beef), *kroepoek* (shrimp crackers), *sateh* (pork kebabs in spicy peanut sauce) and *gado-gado* (vegetables in peanut sauce).

Cheese

Round Edam and cylindrical Gouda cheeses are the best known. Try also *Leidse kaas*, flavoured with caraway seeds, and *Friese kaas*, flavoured with cloves.

Time for a 'knock on the head' – jenever with beer

Drinks

Dutch pilsener beers Heineken, Grolsch and Amstel are well known, and there are others, such as Oranjeboom, Bavaria, Brand, Gulpen, Ridder, Leeuw, Alfa and Lindeboom. For a change, try a *witbier* (white beer) such as Wiekse Witte, or a brown *bokbier*. Dutch *jenever* (gin), usually ordered as a *borrel tje* (small tot), is a popular accompaniment to beer, the two forming a symbiotic relationship called a *kopstoot* ('knock on the head').

40B4
Between Prinsengracht,
Brouwersgracht,
Lijnbaansgracht and
Leidsegracht
1, 2, 5, 13, 14, 17, 20
Museum Boat stop 2

Above: over the hump on a bridge spanning Keizersgracht

40B4
Bars, cafés and
restaurants (€–€€€)
1, 2, 4, 5, 13, 14, 16, 17,
20, 24, 25
Museum Boat stop 2

DE JORDAAN   ✪✪

The Jordaan, which lies west of the centre between Prinsengracht, Brouwersgracht, Singelgracht and Leidsegracht, is a town within a town, built for Golden Age artisans and tradesmen who provided services to their 'betters' on the adjacent *grachtengordel*. Its houses are smaller and more crammed together, its waterways narrower and less grand, than those of the prestigious ring canals. The name may come from the French *jardin*, after the gardens of Protestant Huguenot refugees who lived in the area. Though infiltrated by gentrifiers, the neighbourhood retains a sense of place, and its iconoclastic working-class attitudes have been complemented by an influx of artists, designers and offbeat folks in general. With few 'sights' in the accepted sense, the Jordaan is worth visiting for its character, cafés and restaurants and individualistic shops.

KEIZERSGRACHT   ✪✪✪

The Emperor's Canal is named for Emperor Maximilian of Austria, whose crown graces the Westerkerk spire (➤ 26), and has a wealth of gable and façade styles. Its 2.8km course takes in several sights that merit a close-up look. In its northern reaches, at Nos 40–4, are the Groenland Pakhuizen from 1641, three surviving warehouses from the original five in which the Greenland Company stored whale oil. Number 123, the Huis met de Hoofden, has six sculpted heads on the façade, representing Greek gods. Near the canal's southern end is the Museum Van Loon (➤ 59).

The Jordaan

Listen for the Westerkerk carillon (➤ 26), a reassuring sound that has wafted over the Jordaan for centuries.

Pass the Anne Frankhuis (➤ 17) on Prinsengracht, cross the canal by the first bridge, and backtrack to Bloemgracht.

Check out three 1640s step gables at Nos 87–91, on which are carved gablestones with images of a townsman, countryman and seaman.

Take Eerste Leliedwarsstraat to Egelantiersgracht.

The hardware store at Nos 2–6 is a 1920s Amsterdam School interloper. At Nos 107–45, step through a Delft blue-tiled corridor into the 1617 Sint-Andrieshofje's courtyard garden (➤ 70), an 'oasis of peace'.

Take Eerste Egelantiersdwarsstraat to the corner of Egelantiersstraat, for the Claes Claeszoon Hofje (➤ 43). Continue on Eerste Tuindwarsstraat and Eerste Anjeliersdwarsstraat to Westerstraat.

If you are here when the Westermarkt street market is on, rummage for cheap clothes, records or household items.

Continue on Tweede Boomdwarsstraat, then turn left into Karthuizersstraat.

Numbers 11–19 are 18th-century gabled houses. The Huiszitten Weduwenhof (Nos 69–191) is a former 18th-century home for widows, with a beautiful courtyard garden. A Carthusian monastery used to stand near by.

Come out on to Lindengracht.

Visit the 1670 Suyckerhofje at Nos 149–163, and its beautifully restored courtyard garden.

Take Tweede Goudsbloemdwarsstraat, Palmdwarsstraat and Driehoekstraat to the junction of Brouwersgracht and Singelgracht.

Tranquil Egelantiersgracht – one of the Jordaan's handsome side-canals

Distance
3km

Time
1½ hours

Start point
Westermarkt
✚ 40B4
🚊 13, 14, 17, 20

End point
Singelgracht
✚ 40C4
🚊 3

Lunch
De Prins (➤ 96)
Rum Runners (➤ 96)
't Smalle (➤ 114)

Westermarkt market
🕐 Mon–Sat 9–5

Almost an original: the wax model of Vincent van Gogh at Madame Tussaud's

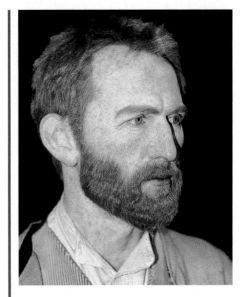

KONINKLIJK PALEIS (► 19, TOP TEN)

LEIDSEPLEIN (► 20, TOP TEN)

- ✚ 40C3
- ✉ Dam 20
- ☎ 622 9239
- ⏱ Mid-Jul–Aug daily 9:30–7:30; Sep–mid-Jul daily 10–5:30. Closed 30 Apr
- 🚌 4, 9, 14, 16, 20, 24, 25
- ♿ Good
- 👍 Very expensive

MADAME TUSSAUD'S   ★★

More than a gallery of waxen Dutch stares, this waxworks uses audio-animatronics, climate-control, smell generators and other special effects to bring to life Holland from the Golden Age onwards. You will see Rembrandt, Vermeer, Jan Steen and others at work. Kings, princes, merchants and peasants put in an appearance. Walk-through scenes include an Amsterdam canalside, a brown café and ice-skating, and there are such famous Dutch characters as Erasmus, Mata Hari and Johann Cruyff, as well as international greats, including Churchill, Einstein and Gandhi.

DID YOU KNOW?

No other city in the world has as many bridges as Amsterdam, which has 1,281. You can see 15 from the bridge over Herengracht at Thorbeckeplein. Torensluis (1684), on Singel at Oude Leliestraat, is the widest. The cast-iron Blauwbrug (Blue Bridge) over the Amstel, built in 1884 and inspired by Paris's Pont Alexandre III, retains the nickname of a 16th-century wooden bridge painted 'Nassau Blue' after the 1578 religious Alteratie; having lost its blue paint in 1969, the Blauwbrug got it back in a renovation completed in 2000.

MAGERE BRUG

The famous 'Skinny Bridge', a white-painted double-drawbridge, has spanned the River Amstel since 1672. The current bridge is a 1969 replacement of an 18th-century enlargement of the original, which is said to have taken its name from two wealthy sisters, called Mager, who lived on opposite banks of the Amstel and who had the bridge built to make it easier for them to visit each other. Its name more likely comes from the original bridge being so narrow that two people could barely cross at the same time. The not-so-skinny footbridge, made of African azobe wood, is the finest of the city's 60 traditional Dutch drawbridges and a big tourist draw at night, when it is lit by hundreds of lights. You might see the bicycle-borne bridge master raising it to let boats through.

41D2
Between Kerkstraat and Nieuwe Kerkstraat
4

Above: *crossing the Amstel on the famous Magere Brug*

MUNTTOREN

The Mint Tower's base is all that remains of the 1490 Reguliers Gate in the demolished city wall. It got its present name in 1672–3, during the war with England and France, when coins were minted here. In 1620, Hendrick de Keyser, who had already topped the Montelbaanstoren, added an ornate, lead-covered spire. A tinkling carillon breaks every hour into classical, folk or pop music, and on Friday from noon until 1PM the bells play a mini-concert. The tower is closed to the public except for a ground-floor shop selling blue porcelain.

Look for a carving on the attached building, which was once a guardhouse and is now a souvenir shop, depicting Amsterdam's alternative foundation tale: the image of two men and a seasick dog in a boat (► 44).

40C3
Muntplein
4, 9, 14, 16, 20, 24, 25
 Museum Boat 4

The hidden splendour of the Church of Our Lord in the Attic

✚ 41D4
✉ Oudezijds Voorburgwal 40
☎ 624 6604
🕐 Mon–Sat 10–5, Sun and pub hols 1–5. Closed 1 Jan, 30 Apr
🚊 4, 9, 14, 16, 20, 24, 25
🚤 Museum Boat stop 1
♿ None
💷 Moderate

MUSEUM AMSTELKRING ✪✪

You get two museums in one here. First is the canal house, built between 1661 and 1663 by merchant Jan Hartman, who sold stockings in a ground-floor shop. Its 17th-century oak furniture, paintings and decoration give a superb idea of period life. Hartman was Catholic and, as a 1578 law prohibited Catholic services, he turned the attics of this and two adjacent houses he also owned into a *schuilkerk*, a clandestine church. Of many such churches, only this one has been completely preserved. Historians of the Amstelkring (Amstel Circle) saved it from demolition in 1888 and named it Ons' Lieve Heer op Solder (Our Lord in the Attic). You climb a narrow stairway to the third-floor church, remodelled in baroque style in 1739 and with many of its original religious objects, including Jacob de Wit's painting *The Baptism of Christ* (1736). An occasional service is still held, as are recitals.

✚ 41D3
✉ Jodenbreestraat 4–6
☎ 520 0400
🕐 Mon–Sat 10–5. Sun and Pub hols 1–5. Closed 1 Jan
🚇 Waterlooplein
🚊 9, 14, 20
🚤 Museum Boat stop 5
♿ Few
💷 Moderate

MUSEUM HET REMBRANDTHUIS ✪✪✪

The great Dutch artist Rembrandt van Rijn (1606–69) owned this house (built in 1606) from 1639, when his work was in constant demand, until he was forced to sell in 1658 because of bankruptcy. Restoration work, completed in 2001, has returned the house to the way it looked when Rembrandt lived and worked in it. The combined living room and bedroom, and Rembrandt's studio are highlights of the tour. His wife, Saskia van Uylenburgh, died here in 1642, aged 30, shortly after their son Titus was born in the house. You can also see paintings by his teacher, Pieter Lastman, and some of his students. Around 250 of Rembrandt's 300 surviving engravings and drawings are on display in the exhibition wing from 1998 next door, including portraits, self-portraits and landscapes.

Rembrandt's house is
now a museum

MUSEUM VAN LOON ✪✪

Along with its neighbouring twin at No 674, this classical mansion of the fading Golden Age by architect Adriaan Dortsman was built between 1671 and 1672 for two wealthy merchant brothers. Rembrandt's student, the artist Ferdinand Bol (1616–80), lived here. The Van Loon family, whose ancestors had played a distinguished role in Holland's history, bought the house in 1884, transforming it into a museum in the 1960s. You can visit its magnificently furnished rooms, climb the marble staircase, stroll in the garden and admire a coach house in the shape of a Greek temple.

✚ 40C2
✉ Keizersgracht 672
☎ 624 5255
🕐 Fri–Mon 11–5. Closed
    1 Jan, 30 Apr, 25 Dec
🚌 6, 24, 25
♿ None
💷 Moderate

MUSEUM WILLET-HOLTHUYSEN ✪✪

Another patrician canal house-turned-museum, this one was built in 1687 for a member of the city council, Jacob Hop. In 1855 Pieter Gerard Holthuysen, a glass merchant, bought it and, in due course, his daughter Sandrina and her husband, Abraham Willett, inherited the house. The couple built up a valuable collection of glass, silver, porcelain and paintings and in 1895 turned over the lot, house included, to an unenthusiastic city council for use as a museum. Following recent refurbishment the museum has been attracting more visitors to its 18th-century basement kitchen, Victorian bedrooms, the Blue Room, with its painted ceiling – *Dawn Chasing Away Night*, by Jacob de Wit (1744) – and dining salon with places set for a banquet.

✚ 41D2
✉ Herengracht 605
☎ 523 1822
🕐 Mon–Fri 10–5, Sat–Sun
    11–5. Closed 1 Jan, 30
    April, 25 Dec
🚌 4, 9, 14, 20
🚤 Museum Boat stop 6
♿ None
💷 Moderate

The full-size replica of the Dutch East Indiaman *Amsterdam,* moored to a wharf at the Netherlands Maritime Museum

✚ 40C3
✉ Dam
🚌 4, 9, 14, 16, 20, 24, 25

✚ 40A1
✉ Vondelpark 3
☎ 589 1400
🕐 Tue–Fri 10–5, Sat 11–5
🍴 Café Vertigo (€€)
🚌 1, 2, 3, 5, 6, 12, 20
🚤 Museum Boat stop 3
♿ Good   Moderate

✚ 41E3
✉ Kattenburgerplein 1
☎ 523 2222
🕐 Tue–Sun 10–5, also Mon
mid-Jun–mid-Sep, School
and pub hols 10–5.
Closed 1 Jan, 30 Apr, 25
Dec
🍴 Café (€)
🚌 Bus 22, 32
🚤 Museum Boat stop 6
♿ Very good
  Expensive

NATIONAAL MONUMENT

The National Monument, an obelisk with symbolic sculptures, was erected in 1956 to commemorate the victims of Holland's occupation by Nazi Germany during World War II. Over the years it has become a popular meeting place. A German company specialising in conserving natural stone renovated the monument between 1997 and 1998.

NEDERLANDS FILMMUSEUM

At a 19th-century lakeside café-turned-dual-screen cinema in Vondelpark, film buffs get to see the best of historical, avant-garde and international films. Many are from the museum's own 35,000-film collection, and the movies are backed up by an extensive library and intermittent temporary exhibitions.

NEDERLANDS SCHEEPVAARTMUSEUM

The star turn at the Netherlands Maritime Museum is the *Amsterdam* (see box), a full-size replica of a Dutch East India Company sailing ship that ran aground and was lost off Hastings in 1749, which is tied up at the museum's wharf. From April to October its 'crew' puts on regular re-enactments of scenes from an 18th-century sailor's life. The *Amsterdam* has been joined by the *Stad Amsterdam*, a replica 19th-century iron clipper, which is moored at nearby Java Island when it's not sailing. The museum, in a 1656 Amsterdam Admiralty arsenal, is a treasure trove of this seafaring nation's long and distinguished maritime history. In addition to the two replicas you can see an ice-breaker, a lifeboat, a herring lugger, canal barges, Holland's royal barge, last used in 1962 for Queen Juliana's silver wedding anniversary, and Greenpeace's *Rainbow Warrior*, as well as models of sailing ships, liners, warships and modern cargo vessels.

Among historical maps and charts is a bound edition of cartographer Jan Blaeu's 17th-century *World Atlas*, accompanied by marine paintings, navigational instruments, photographs, ships' equipment and other nautical bits and pieces. A particular focus is the history of the Amsterdam-based Verenigde Oostindische Compagnie (United East India Company), founded in 1602.

The 17th-century Amsterdam Admiralty arsenal that houses the Maritime Museum

The hi-tech NEMO

DID YOU KNOW?

When the *Amsterdam* lost its rudder on a voyage to the East Indies, Captain Willem Klump beached his three-masted ship off Hastings in England. He saved his passengers and crew and recovered 28 chests of silver. Much of the cargo remains onboard: medicines, foodstuffs, wine, muskets, cannon and munitions. With its upper decks washed away and its hull visible at very low tide, the *Amsterdam* lies embedded in sand.

NEMO ⭐⭐

Technology and science are the related themes at this interactive museum housed in a spectacular, modern building from 1997 by Italian architect Renzo Piano in Amsterdam harbour. NEMO brings you face to face with the latest developments through such hands-on virtual activities as steering a supertanker, trading shares, generating power and performing surgery. You can conduct scientific experiments in a laboratory, do basic research on natural phenomena, play computer games, watch tech-oriented demonstrations, movies and theatre performances, listen to debates, surf the web and tour temporary exhibitions. The rooftop terrace has become a popular spot for watching the sunset.

🔲 41E4
✉ Oosterdok 2
☎ 0900 919 1100
🕐 Tue–Sun 10–5; Mon 10–5 during school hols. Closed 1 Jan, 30 Apr, 25 Dec
🍽 Café with waterside terrace (€); cafeteria with rooftop terrace (€–€€)
🚌 Bus 22, 32
🚢 Museum Boat stop 6
♿ Very good
💶 Very expensive

Refurbished and revived, Nieuwmarkt is awash with restaurants and cafés

---

NIEUWE KERK

The New Church has been Holland's coronation church since 1815, but is now mostly used for art exhibitions and cultural events. It dates from 1408, though an original Gothic structure was destroyed by fire in 1521. Calvinists stripped out the Catholic ornamentation after their 1578 take-over. Where the high altar once stood is an elaborate marble memorial to Admiral Michiel de Ruyter (1607–76), who in 1667 singed the King of England's beard by sailing up the Medway and destroying an English fleet. Sculpted by Rombout Verhulst, it depicts the hero lying on a cannon, surrounded by sea creatures. Poets Pieter Cornelisz Hooft (1581–1647) and Joost van den Vondel (1587–1679) are buried in the church in unmarked graves.

NIEUWMARKT

A seedy area well into the 1980s, where heroin addicts and ne'er-do-wells hung out. One street leading off the square, Zeedijk, was a notorious shooting gallery and others led into rough parts of the red-light district. Its character was appropriate, as this was once the site of public executions, and bits and pieces of dismembered criminals were hung up on De Waag (➤ 73) as a warning to others. Having been cleaned up, more or less, it is becoming a popular, alternative nightlife zone. At the heart of the city's Chinatown, it has many authentic, inexpensive Chinese eateries, as well as good traditional Dutch cafés with pavement terraces.

NOORDERKERK ✪

The austere North Church, renovated between 1997 and 1998, is a rarity in this nominally Calvinist city: a Calvinist church with a substantial congregation. It was built in the shape of a Greek cross by Hendrick de Keyser, and completed in 1623 by Hendrick Staets after De Keyser's death in 1621. Staets tucked four little triangular houses into the angles of the cross.

Surrounding Noordermarkt hosts a bird market and organic food market on Saturday with stalls selling fruit and vegetables, herbs and cheeses, and a flea market on Monday.

✚ 40B4
✉ Noordermarkt 44–8
☎ 626 6436
🕐 Sat 11–1 (followed by chamber music concert 1–2), Sun services 10AM and 7PM, Mon 10:30–12:30. Closed Tue–Fri
🚌 Bus 18, 22
♿ Few
💶 Free

OOSTINDISCH HUIS ✪

This is the former headquarters of the once-powerful Verenigde Oostindische Compagnie (United East India Company), which was founded in 1602. Its occupants once sent expeditions to the Orient to bring back silks, spices and other riches that fuelled Amsterdam's Golden Age. They controlled their own army and had authority to declare war and make treaties. Hendrick de Keyser's red brick and yellow sandstone building, dating from 1605–6, now belongs to Amsterdam University; you can stroll into its courtyard.

✚ 41D3
✉ Oude Hoogstraat 24
🚌 4, 9, 14, 16, 20, 24, 25

Oude Kerk is an island of piety in the Red Light District

OUDE KERK ✪✪

The Gothic Old Church, begun in 1334, stands in the heart of the Red Light District, surrounded by former almshouses. In summer you can climb the spire, built by Joost Bilhamer in 1555, and on Saturday between 4 and 5PM the carillon bursts into tune. Not much Catholic ornamentation survived the Calvinist takeover, but in the Mariakapel you can see three superb stained-glass windows. Composer Jan Sweelinck (1562–1621) is buried in the church where he was organist for 45 years, as are Rembrandt's wife Saskia, a squadron of 17th-century admirals and poet Maria Tesselschade, who died in 1649.

✚ 41D4
✉ Oudekerksplein 23
☎ 625 8284
🕐 Apr–Oct Mon–Sat 11–5, Sun 1–5; Nov–Mar Sun–Fri 1–5, Sat 11–5. Closed 1 Jan, 30 Apr
🚇 Nieuwmarkt
🚌 4, 9, 14, 16, 20, 24, 25
♿ Good
💶 Moderate

63

Old Centre

Distance
3km

Time
2 hours

Start point
Rokin, at Spui
✚ 40C3
🚊 4, 9, 14, 16, 20, 24, 25

End point
Dam
✚ 40C3
🚊 4, 9, 14, 16, 20, 24, 25

Lunch
Café Roux (➤ 93)
La Ruche (➤ 96)

The Oude Kerk organ, once played by composer Jan Sweelinck

Flirt with the salacious on a stroll through De Wallen, and find there is more to the oldest part of town than sleaze.

Walk past a canal boat dock and a statue of Queen Wilhelmina, into Lange Brugsteeg and Grimburgwal, to Oudezijds Voorburgwal.

You are on Amsterdam University's downtown campus. Across the canal is a 16th-century red-brick, step-gabled house with a view of three canals. To your left, on Oudezijds Voorburgwal, is the Athenaeum Illustre (➤ 38).

Cross over the canal to Oudezijds Achterburg-wal. Directly ahead is Oudemanhuispoort, a covered passage lined with second-hand book shops (➤ 65). Go through and turn left on Kloveniersburgwal.

Across the water, at No 95, you see the neo-classical Poppenhuis, built in the 1640s for merchant Joan Poppen.

Continue to Oude Hoogstraat and turn left to visit the courtyard of Oostindisch Huis (➤ 63). Return to Kloveniersburgwal and turn left.

Across the water, at No 29, is the neo-classical Trippen-huis, built between 1660 and 1664 by Justus Vingboons for the arms merchant Trip brothers – with chimneys shaped like cannon barrels. It is actually two houses, one for each of the brothers, disguised by false middle windows to maintain its symmetry. The building is now home to the Netherlands Academy. You pass tiny Klein-Trippenhuis, built for their coachman, at No 26 (➤ 71).

Keep going to Nieuwmarkt and De Waag (➤ 73). Take Zeedijk, then turn left on Molensteeg into the heart of the Red Light District (➤ 21). Keep going across the two canals until you come to the Oude Kerk (➤ 63).

Prostitutes' red-lit windows surround the church.

Take Wijde Kerksteeg, then turn left on Warmoesstraat, to the Dam.

OUDEMANHUISPOORT ✪

Once the entrance to a hospice for elderly men, this long covered passage dating from 1601 beside Amsterdam University now houses antiquarian and second-hand book shops that spread their wares on tables lining the arcade. Midway along, on either side, are doors that open onto Amsterdam University's law department buildings; the doors on the left lead first to a courtyard garden with a sculpted head of Minerva in the middle.

🔲 40C3
🕐 Mon–Sat 10–5/6
🚊 4, 9, 14, 16, 20, 24, 25

PORTUGEES-ISRAËLIETISCHE SYNAGOGE ✪

Sephardic Jews fleeing persecution in Spain and Portugal began to settle in Amsterdam during the 1580s, bringing a touch of colour to the sober, Calvinist city. As a sign of their prosperity in a tolerant environment, they pooled their wealth to build the lavish Portuguese-Israelite Synagogue (1671–5), designed by Elias Bouman. Wooden barrel vaults supported on Ionic columns form the interior, which is decorated with low-hanging brass chandeliers.

🔲 41D3
✉ Mr Visserplein 1
☎ 624 5351
🕐 Sun–Fri 10–4 (Nov–Mar Fri 10–3). Closed Sat & Jewish hols (except for services)
Ⓜ Waterlooplein
🚊 9, 14, 20
⛴ Museum Boat stop 5
♿ Good
💰 Moderate

Knick-knacks and souvenir shops on Prinsengracht

PRINSENGRACHT ✪✪✪

Prinsengracht, the outermost of the three concentric ring canals, was named after Prince William of Orange. It was dug in the 17th century to house shopkeepers and craftsmen. With the stiffly formal patricians' and merchants' houses reserved for Herengracht (► 47) and Keizersgracht (► 54), Prinsengracht's down-to-earth style has survived the centuries. A stroll along its houseboat-lined, 3.5km length and into adjacent side-streets, particularly in the northern section bordering the Jordaan (► 54), takes you past cosy brown cafés, notable restaurants and offbeat shops and boutiques. Highlights of its course through the city are the Anne Frankhuis (► 17) and Westerkerk (► 26); also visit the Noorderkerk (► 63) and the canal's junction with Brouwersgracht (► 42).

🔲 40B4
🍴 Many cafés and restaurants (€–€€€)
🚊 1, 2, 4, 5, 7, 10, 13, 14, 16, 17, 20, 24, 25
⛴ Museum Boat stop 2

PRINSENHOF

The Prince's House was the St Cecilia Convent until the 1578 Protestant Alteratie, when the city commandeered it as a lodging house. In 1647, the Admiralty moved in, and when, in 1808, Louis Napoleon turfed the city councillors out of their town hall on the Dam, they moved here. Since the council left in 1986, the Prinsenhof has become the Grand Hotel, a predominantly 1920s Amsterdam School structure. In its Café Roux (➤ 93), you can see a 1949 mural, *Inquisitive Children*, by Cobra artist Karel Appel.

RED LIGHT DISTRICT (➤ 21, TOP TEN)

REMBRANDTPLEIN

Brash and bustling Rembrandtplein jumps at night with music from the mostly unmemorable cafés that surround it (see side panel for three exceptions). A bronze statue of Rembrandt (1852) by Louis Royer, in the middle of the square, doesn't look much like the down-at-heel self-portraits the artist typically painted. While you're here, visit the magnificent, art deco Tuschinski Cinema (1921) in adjacent Reguliersbreestraat 26 – you can wander around the lobby, and in July and August join guided tours.

Rembrandt occupies pride of place in the square that bears his name

DE RIEKER ✪

Amsterdam's finest windmill stands amid idyllic surroundings beside the River Amstel and Amstelpark (▶ 33) in the city's leafy southern outskirts. Built in 1636 to drain the Rieker polder (low-lying reclaimed land), the windmill was moved here in the 1970s. It has been beautifully preserved and is now a private home. Rembrandt used to walk in this area after his wife's death, sketching and painting riverside scenes, and a statue of the artist at work stands beside the windmill.

RIJKSMUSEUM (▶ 22–3, TOP TEN)

RONDVAARTBOTEN ✪✪✪

Seventy tour boats ply Amsterdam's canals, carrying 2.5 million passengers a year. Many visitors prefer not to board a canal boat. Don't be one of them. True, there's a lot of tourist hokum associated with these glass-topped cruisers but you can ignore that, more or less, and focus on the unmatched view you get of this canal-threaded city from the water, gliding past a parade of Golden Age gables enlivened by contemporary bustle and colour.

Nine tour-boat companies (▶ side panel) sail from jetties around the city centre – at Centraal Station, along Damrak and Rokin, at Leidseplein and on Singelgracht at Weteringplantsoen.

Most cruises last about an hour and follow a similar pattern: through the ring canals and the old city, around the Red Light District, taking in the River Amstel and a circuit of Centraal Station along the way. There are longer cruises on the river and through the old harbour, as well as dinner- and cheese-and-wine-cruises.

Variations on the tour boat theme are the Canal Bus, Museumboat and water-taxis, as well as 'saloon boat' tours on refurbished motor launches dating from the 1890s to the 1920s. And although it's not quite the same thing, you can be captain of your own 'ship' and tour the waterways by water bike (▶ 42). Remember that boat traffic keeps to the right-hand side of the canal.

🔢 29D1
✉ Corner of Amsteldijk and De Borcht
🍴 't Klein Kalfje (▶ 94)
🚌 Bus 148

❓ Canal boat tours are operated by:
Amsterdam Canal Cruises ☎ 626 5636
Holland International ☎ 622 7788
Meijers Rondvaarten ☎ 623 4208
Rederij Boekel ☎ 612 9905
Rederij Hof van Holland ☎ 623 7122
Rederij Lovers ☎ 530 1090
Rederij Noord-Zuid ☎ 679 1370
Rederij P Kooij ☎ 623 3810
Rederij Plas ☎ 624 5406

Cruiseboat is the best way to travel

*From shipping company
headquarters to city
transport offices –
Scheepvaarthuis*

✚ 41D4
✉ Prins Hendrikkade
108–114
🕐 Mon–Fri 9–4:30
🚇 Centraal Station
🚌 22, 32, 33, 34, 35, 39
🛥 Museum Boat stop 1

SCHEEPVAARTHUIS

Maritime House, noted for its curving lines and marine
motifs, is a work of the Amsterdam School, which
flowered briefly early this century. Designed by Michel de
Klerk, Pieter Kramer and Johan van der May between 1912
and 1913 for a consortium of local shipping companies, it
now houses the city's municipal transport authority, the
GVB. It is ornamented with portrait busts of famous
captains, navigators and cartographers. Beside it, at Prins
Hendrikkade 131, is a house that once belonged to the
17th-century admiral, Michiel de Ruyter.

✚ 41D4
✉ Prins Hendrikkade 94–5
🚇 Centraal Station
🚊 Tram 1, 2, 4, 5, 9, 13, 16,
17, 20, 24, 25; bus 22, 32
🛥 Museum Boat stop 1

SCHREIERSTOREN

The Weeping Tower began life around 1480 as a heavily
fortified strong point in the city wall overlooking the
harbour. Its somewhat fanciful name comes from the tears
sailors' wives and sweethearts ostensibly shed from its
ramparts as ships sailed away on long and often fatal
voyages to the East and West Indies. A plaque on the wall
shows such an apparently distraught woman watching a
ship depart. Other plaques on the tower record Henry
Hudson's 1609 voyage to what was to be known as New
York and the Hudson River, and Cornelis Houtman's 1595
voyage to Indonesia; both expeditions left from the
harbour here.

✚ 40C3
✉ Kalverstraat 92,
Nieuwezijds Voorburgwal
359, Sint Luciënsteeg 27
☎ 523 1822
🕐 Mon–Fri 10–5, Sat–Sun
and pub hols 11–5
🚊 1, 2, 4, 5, 9, 14, 16, 20,
24, 25
🛥 Museum Boat stop 4
♿ Very good 💷 Free

SCHUTTERSGALERIJ

The Civic Guards Gallery, belonging to the Amsterdams
Historisch Museum (▶ 16), displays 15 vast 16th- and
17th-century group portraits of the city's Civic Guards, local
militia companies. They are hung in a covered passageway
that was once a narrow canal separating the boys' and
girls' courtyards of the former orphanage (now housing the
Historical Museum). One of the canvases on display is
*Joan Huydecoper's Militia Celebrating the Peace of
Münster* (1648), which was painted by Rembrandt's
student Govert Flinck.

SEXMUSEUM AMSTERDAM VENUSTEMPEL ✪

The Venus Temple allusion is bolstered by a false marble entrance in the shape of a classical pediment. Once past the 'cultural' stuff, you're into the Sex Museum's serious business, which ranges from naughty to downright dirty. Erotic photographs and videos show practitioners at work on diverse forms of interpersonal relationships. Mannequins are used to bring you close to the 'action'. Other exhibits include toys, trinkets, specialised clothing and appliances.

SINGEL ✪✪✪

Before the city embarked on its Golden Age expansion, this canal formed a moat outside the walls. By the early 17th century it was a residential zone and the earliest ring canal. There are few major monuments on its 1.7km course through the city between Prins Hendrikkade, near Centraal Station, and the Munttoren (► 57), beside the Flower Market (► 39), yet a stroll along its length is full of minor interest. The Nieuwe Haarlemmersluis beside Brouwersgracht, an outlet from the canals, plays an important part in the 1½-hour 'enema' the system gets every night, when fresh water is pumped through to flush the canals out. Near here, at Singel 40, is the *Poezenboot*, a houseboat-refuge for dozens of stray cats. The Torensluis at Oude Leliestraat is the city's widest bridge.

Among Singel's most interesting churches is the Ronde Lutherse Koepelkerk (Round Domed Lutheran Church), built between 1668 and 1671 by Adriaen Dortsman for the city's Lutheran community and now used by the Renaissance Amsterdam Hotel as a conference centre.

✚ 41D4
✉ Damrak 18
☎ 622 8376
🕐 Daily 10AM–11:30PM
🚉 Centraal Station
🚌 1, 2, 4, 5, 9, 13, 16, 17, 20, 24, 25
🚤 Museum Boat stop 4
♿ Few   💰 Inexpensive
❓ No admission to under-16s

✚ 40C4
🍴 Cafés and restaurants (€–€€€)
🚌 1, 2, 4, 5, 9, 13, 14, 16, 17, 20, 24, 25
🚤 Museum Boat stop 1, 4

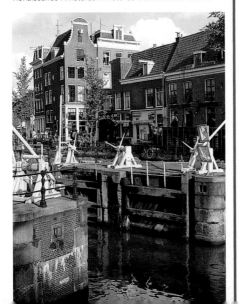

Nieuwe Haarlemmersluis gives access to and from the Singel

40C4
Tram 1, 2, 5, 13, 17, 20
Museum Boat stop 1

SINGEL 7 ✪
Canal boat tour guides point out the façade of this 16th-century house as the city's narrowest, at 1m wide – an important consideration in times past, as the wider the canal frontage, the more a building cost. Singel 7 cleverly uses a narrow frontage then widens to a more usual size behind the façade.

40B4
Egelantiersgracht 107–45
7, 10, 17, 20

SINT-ANDRIESHOFJE ✪
Bequeathed in 1615–17 by cattle farmer Ivo Gerrittszoon, this restored almshouse still forms a social housing unit. A corridor lined with Delft blue tiles leads to a courtyard garden, filled with flowers and containing a water pump and a dedication stone with the legend *Vrede Sy Met U* (Peace Be With You).

41D4
Prins Hendrikkade 73
624 8749
Mon–Sat 11–4; Sun services
Centraal Station
1, 2, 4, 5, 9, 13, 16, 17, 20, 24, 25
Museum Boat stop 1
Good
Free

Puzzling over the meanings at the modern art Stedelijk Museum

SINT-NICOLAASKERK ✪
With its twin towers and tall, domed cupola, the city's main Catholic church (1888), dedicated to St Nicholas, is a highly visible landmark facing Centraal Station. Recently restored, the church's richly decorated interior is almost neo-baroque, its square pillars topped with Corinthian capitals. The marble high altar is flanked by bronze reliefs recalling the 1345 Miracle of Amsterdam: on the right Emperor Maximilian gives Amsterdam the imperial crown after being cured of illness following a visit to the Sacrament Chapel; on the left is a depiction of the Miracle Procession. In addition to being the patron saint of sailors, St Nicholas is Sinterklaas, Holland's traditional version of Santa Claus, who on the night of 5 December – *Sinterklaasavond*, or *Pakjesavond* – delivers presents to sleeping children.

STEDELIJK MUSEUM ✪✪✪

The Municipal Museum opened in 1895 as a storehouse for knick-knacks collected by eccentric maid-turned-millionairess Sophia Lopez-Suasso, most of which went out the door in 1945 when director Willem Sandberg reinvented it as a modern art museum. A new wing opened in 1954 and another extension, on Museumplein, is planned. Things change fast at the Stedelijk and you never know what will be on view. The permanent collection includes De Stijl works by Piet Mondrian, Cobra by Karel Appel and abstract expressionism by Willem de Kooning. Among many other artists represented are Calder, Cézanne, Chagall, Manet, Monet, Oldenburg, Picasso, Renoir, Rosenquist, Van Gogh and Warhol, and there's also a large collection of abstract paintings by Russian artist Kasimir Malevich. There is strong public demand to view the Stedelijk's works from around 1900 until the 1970s, while the healthy private galleries scene in the city allows the very latest art to be viewed elsewhere.

+ 40B1
✉ Paulus Potterstraat 13
☎ 573 2911
🕐 Daily 11–5. Closed 1 Jan, 30 Apr, 25 Dec
🍴 Café-restaurant (€–€€)
🚃 2, 3, 5, 12, 16, 20
⛴ Museum Boat stop 3
♿ Very good
✋ Moderate

STEDELIJK MUSEUM BUREAU AMSTERDAM ✪

The decision by the Stedelijk Museum to focus on displaying modern art up to about the 1970s has left space in its coverage – or a window of opportunity – between that decade and the present which this 'offspring' gallery is designed to fill. It does so by focusing on contemporary painting, sculpture, video works, installations and performance art, mainly by young Amsterdam artists.

+ B4
✉ Rozenstraat 59
☎ 422 0471
🕐 Tue–Sun, pub hols 11–5. Closed 1 Jan, 30 Apr, 25 Dec
🚃 13, 14, 17, 20
♿ Moderate
✋ Free

DID YOU KNOW?

The Klein Trippenhuis at Kloveniersburgwal 26, which has a façade 2.44m wide, was built in 1696 for the coachman of the merchant Trip brothers (▶ 64), whose own house, at Kloveniersburgwal 29, is 22m wide. One of the brothers apparently overheard the coachman saying how he wished he had a house as wide as his masters' door, and the lucky servant had his wish fulfilled. Nowadays it's a trendy fashion boutique.

Above: *modern sculpture outside the Stedelijk Museum*

Costume pieces take centre stage at the Theatermuseum

THEATERMUSEUM ✪✪

Housed in a 1638 canalside mansion designed by Philips Vingboons, with 18th-century painted ceilings by Jacob de Wit and other artists, the museum is a storehouse of Dutch and international theatre, as well as a fine example of a patrician canal house. You can see a miniature stage, costumes, models, masks, puppets, photographs, paintings and theatrical backdrops. The Netherlands Theatre Institute occupies offices in the adjacent four canal houses, including the Bartolotti House at No 170–2, built in 1618 by Hendrick de Keyser, which also has ceilings by De Wit and others.

✚ 40C4
✉ Herengracht 168
☎ 551 3300
🕐 Tue–Fri 11–5, Sat–Sun & pub hols 1–5. Closed 1 Jan, 30 Apr, 25 Dec
🍴 Café (€)
🚋 13, 14, 17, 20
🚤 Museum Boat stop 2
♿ Few
💶 Moderate

TORENSLUIS ✪

The widest bridge in the old town stands on the site of a 17th-century sluice gate flanked by twin towers that were demolished in 1829. Its foundations were used for what must have been a particularly damp and gloomy prison. Today, outdoor terraces encroach onto the bridge from nearby cafés. The bronze statue is of Multatuli (Eduard Douwes Dekker), a 19th-century author.

✚ C4
✉ Singel (at Oude Leliestraat)
🚋 1, 2, 5, 13, 17, 20

TRAMMUSEUM AMSTERDAM ✪

Not only has this museum, housed in the old Haarlemmermeerstation, preserved some of Amsterdam's antique trams, it has also gathered up venerable trams from other European cities. On Sundays in summer, one of these old bone-shakers sees action on the Museum Tramlijn, a 6km line that runs from the station southwards through Amsterdamse Bos (▶ 33) to Bovenkerk.

✚ 28C2
✉ Amstelveenseweg 264
☎ 673 7538
🕐 Easter–Aug Sun and pub hols 10:30–5:20; Jun–Jul also Sat 8–10PM
🚋 6, 16 ♿ None
💶 Moderate

TROPENMUSEUM ✪✪✪

You might not be surprised to hear an Indonesian gamelan orchestra in Amsterdam – Indonesia was a Dutch colony, after all – but how about visiting an Arab bazaar, a Bombay slum or a Bangladeshi village? You will find them all, and more, at the outstanding Tropical Museum. Though built between 1916 and 1926 as a paean of praise to Holland's empire in the East and West Indies, in the 1970s it refocused on culture, crafts and environment in the developing world. A hands-on, walk-through, realistic style makes for a fun-filled and educational day out. Imaginative temporary exhibitions and performances of non-Western music are held in the lofty, galleried main hall. Visiting the Kindermuseum gives six- to 12-year-olds an insight into how people from other cultures live.

🚩 41F2
✉ Linnaeusstraat 2
☎ 568 8200; Kindermuseum (reservations recommended) 568 8233
🕐 Daily 10–5. Closed 1 Jan, 30 Apr, 5 May, 25 Dec.
🍴 Café-restaurant Ekeko (€–€€)
🚌 3, 6, 7, 9, 10, 14
♿ Very good
💶 Expensive

VAN GOGH MUSEUM (▶ 24, TOP TEN)

VONDELPARK (▶ 25, TOP TEN)

Above: *exhibits from far-flung places at the Tropenmuseum*

WAAG ✪

Built in 1488, the moated and fortified Sint-Antoniespoort gateway in the city walls was converted into a weigh-house and guild headquarters in 1617. Rembrandt's *The Anatomy Lesson of Dr Tulp* (1632), depicting a dissection by Surgeon's Guild members, was painted here in the preserved upper floor Theatrum Anatomicum. With the city walls long vanished and the moat filled in to form Nieuwmarkt, the Waag now houses a multimedia foundation, and has a fine café-restaurant, Inde Waag, on the ground floor.

🚩 41D3
✉ Nieuwmarkt 4
☎ 557 9898
🕐 Rarely open to the public (except café-restaurant)
🍴 Café-restaurant (▶ 97)
Ⓜ Nieuwmarkt
🚌 4, 9, 14, 16, 20, 24, 25
♿ Few
💶 Free (charge for some exhibitions)

73

Above: *Waterlooplein flea market has all the knick-knacks you need*

WATERLOOPLEIN ★★

Once the heart of Amsterdam's Jewish Quarter, the square and its surroundings have been brutalized by successive 'development' projects since the end of the war, when it lay in ruins. A spark of the old life survives in the Waterlooplein Vlooienmarkt (flea market), which may have lost the legendary colour of its Jewish heyday, but retains the charm intrinsic to a market that retails everything from valuable antiques to worthless trash (▶ 106). The umbilically joined 1980s, postmodern Stadhuis (Town Hall) and Muziektheater (Opera), occupy the centre of the square. Between the two is the Normaal Amsterdams Peil (Amsterdam Ordnance Datum), a bronze plaque that sets Europe's altitude standard; one of the three water-filled glass columns beside it shows the high-water mark of the 1953 Zeeland floods.

WERF 'T KROMHOUT ★

The 18th-century Kromhout Wharf, one of the city's oldest dockyards, and among few still in business, runs a museum alongside its day-to-day operations. The shipyard was founded in the 18th century by Diede Jansen Kromhout. You can watch old canal boats being repaired and see a collection of ship's engines.

WESTERKERK (▶ 26, TOP TEN)

WESTINDISCH HUIS ★

Opened in 1615 as a meat market, in 1623 this became headquarters of the Dutch West India Company, which controlled Holland's trade with the Americas. In the same year the company built a settlement on Manhattan Island and in 1626 founded Nieuw Amsterdam (New York), naming nearby districts after Haarlem (Harlem), Breukelen (Brooklyn) and the Dutch republic's parliament, the Staten-Generaal (Staten Island). A statue of Peter Stuyvesant, Nieuw Amsterdam's governor from 1646 until 1664, stands in the courtyard, and the building now houses the John Adams Institute, a US-orientated literary and philosophical society.

WOONBOOTMUSEUM ✪✪

If you've ever wondered what life is like aboard the city's 2,500 houseboats moored on the canals, the River Amstel and in the harbour, the Houseboat Museum is your chance to find out – though as houseboats are as individual as the people who live on them, it can only be an example rather than typical.

The 23m *Hendrika Maria*, built in 1914, was a working canal barge before being converted to a houseboat. Its hold is now living space, together with the deckhouse where the skipper and his family lived. You can tour these quarters, which have ship models and photographs on view. As with most houseboats, there is no shortage of living space but it's hard to stand up straight.

✚ 40B3
✉ Beside Prinsengracht 296
☎ 427 0750
🕐 Wed–Sun 11–5. Closed 1 Jan, mid-Jan, 30 Apr, 25 Dec
🚊 7, 10, 17, 20
🚤 Museum Boat stop 2
♿ None
🎫 Inexpensive

ZUIDERKERK ✪✪

Built by Hendrick de Keyser between 1603 and 1614, the city's first, new, post-Reformation Protestant church has not been used for religious purposes since 1929. It now houses the municipal town planning information centre and an exhibition on recent and proposed urban development. At certain times you can climb the Italianate church's ornate bell tower for a magnificent view over the Nieuwmarkt and Waterlooplein districts. The churchyard, where Rembrandt's first three children were buried, has been paved over and surrounded by modern apartments, but De Keyser's Renaissance gateway, 'decorated' with carved skulls, still stands beside Sint-Antoniesbreestraat.

✚ 41D3
✉ Zuiderkerkhof 72
☎ 552 7987
🕐 Mon–Wed & Fri 12–5, Thu 12–8. Church tower guided tour: Jun–Sep Wed–Sat 2, 3 & 4PM
🚇 Nieuwmarkt, Waterlooplein
🚊 9, 14, 20
🚤 Museum Boat stop 5
♿ Good
🎫 Free (church tower inexpensive)

Time has run out on Zuiderkerk's religious calling

Excursions from the City

Holland is a small country. From Amsterdam you can reach its furthest mainland extremities in about three hours by way of vigorous driving or an intercity train. Within easy reach of the capital, a variety of excellent excursion options awaits you. A mere 20 minutes by train from Centraal Station is Haarlem, a memorable city in its own right, and it would be hard to imagine urban experiences more varied than those offered by The Hague, Rotterdam and Utrecht. If you need to be beside water you can choose from a string of North Sea beach resorts, such as nearby Zandvoort, or the constellation of historic towns and villages encircling the IJsselmeer lake, the former Zuiderzee. You can tour around by bicycle within a fair radius of the city, or cycle to your chosen place of escape and return by train.

> *'...the Dutch landscape has all the qualities that make geometry so delightful. A tour in Holland is a tour through the first book of Euclid. Over a country that is the ideal plane surface of the geometry books, the roads and the canals trace out the shortest distances between point and point.'*
>
> ALDOUS HUXLEY
> *Along the Road (1925)*

●

The picturesque Kinderdjik windmills near Rotterdam

☒ Legmeerdijk 313,
   Aalsmeer
☎ 0297/392 185
🕐 Mon–Fri 7:30–11. Closed
   1 Jan, 31 Dec (and
   variably on other public
   holidays)
🖐 Moderate

Below: *cheese carriers at
Alkmaar cheese market*

☒ Waagplein
🕐 Mid-Apr to mid-Sep Fri
   10–12

Hollands Kaasmuseum
☒ De Waag, Waagplein 2
☎ 072/511 4284
🕐 Apr–Oct Mon–Thu & Sat
   10–4, Fri 9–4
🖐 Inexpensive

Keukenhof Garden
☒ Stationsweg 166A, Lisse
☎ 0252/465555
🕐 Late Mar–late May daily
   8–6 (visitors in by 6 can
   stay till 7:30); mid-Aug–
   mid-Sep 9–6:30 (visitors
   in by 6:30 can stay till 8)
♿ Very good
🖐 Very expensive

AALSMEER BLOEMENVEILING

Flowers are big business at Aalsmeer's Flower Auction,
12km southwest of Amsterdam, where three billion cut
flowers and 400 million potted plants from 8,000
nurseries, worth 500 million euros, change hands annually.
The bidding process is highly automated and lightning fast.
Dealers sit at consoles in four auditoriums, in front of big
clocks with numbers from 100 to 1 on their dials. As
flower and plant lots move past, the clock hand counts
downwards. The first dealer to press his console button
makes the highest bid, stopping the clock and securing
the lot.

ALKMAAR KAASMARKT

The Cheese Market at Alkmaar, 37km northwest of
Amsterdam, is a slice of Dutch kitsch, but no less
endearing for that. Every Friday morning in summer,
cobblestoned Waagplein is littered with heaps of round
Edam and cylindrical Gouda cheeses ready for auction.
Buyers and sellers taste and haggle, sealing agreements
with a clap of their hands. White-clad *kaasdragers* (cheese-
porters), whose four different guild companies are
identified by red, blue,
yellow and green straw-
hats, put the sold
cheese lots on shoulder-
slung wooden barrows
and run with them to the
Waag (Weigh House), a
14th-century church
converted in 1582. You
can visit the **Hollands
Kaasmuseum** (Dutch
Cheese Museum) in the
Waag.

BOLLENSTREEK AND KEUKENHOF

Tulip mania strikes the Bulb District between Haarlem and
Leiden every spring. Field upon field of tulips stretches to
the wide Dutch horizon. Polders (reclaimed land) become
parade-grounds for a vast army of flowers, lined up in
orderly regiments, each variety identified by its distinctive
colour and shape – with an occasional lost recruit, a speck
of red in a sea of yellow maybe, marooned in the wrong
bunch. You can tiptoe through the tulips on bus tours, boat
tours, taxi tours, train tours, bicycle tours, walking tours
and aerial tours.

   The world-famous **Keukenhof Garden**, near Lisse,

Left: *late spring is the time to come to Keukenhof Garden*

35km southwest of Amsterdam, in the heart of the bulb district, is overrun by 900,000 visitors in a two-month period in spring. These are vastly outnumbered by nearly 6 million flowers, mostly tulips, daffodils and hyacinths, but including other species, planted by Dutch flower growers in a different layout each year to showcase their products and skills.

DELFT ⬤⬤⬤
Home of the painter Jan Vermeer (1632–75) and burial place of Dutch royalty, Delft, 56km southwest of Amsterdam, is a handsome, canal-lined town. Few of its medieval buildings survived a fire in 1536 and a massive explosion at a powder magazine in 1654. Prince William the Silent, who led Holland's revolt against Spain and was assassinated in 1584 at the **Prinsenhof** – now a museum where you can still see bullet holes from the fusillade that killed him – is among members of the House of Oranje-Nassau buried in the 14th-century Nieuwe Kerk. Vermeer is buried in the 13th-century Oude Kerk. You can visit the workshop of **De Koninklijke Porcelyne Fles**, renowned makers of traditional, hand-painted Delft blue porcelain.

> ### DID YOU KNOW?
> German singer-songwriter Klaus-Günter Neumann wrote that quintessentially 'Dutch' song *Tulips from Amsterdam* in 1956. Postcards now take the cliché a step further, by showing a pair of sticky red lips and the slogan 'Two Lips From Amsterdam'.

🛈 Markt 83–5 ☎ 015/213 0100 🕐 Apr–Oct Mon–Sat 9–5:30, Sun 11–3; Nov–Mar Mon–Fri 9–5:30, Sat 9–5

Prinsenhof Museum
✉ St Agathaplein 1
☎ 015/260 2358
🕐 Tue–Sat 10–5, Sun & pub hols 1–5. Closed 1 Jan, 25 Dec
💰 Inexpensive

De Koninklijke Porcelyne Fles
✉ Rotterdamseweg 196
☎ 015/251 2030
🕐 Guided tours Mon–Sat 9–5; also Sun (Apr–late Oct) 9:30–5. Closed 24 Dec–2 Jan
💰 Inexpensive

There's more to Edam than cheese – enjoy a stroll along the elegant canal banks

 Stadhuis, Damplein 1
☎ 0299/315 125
🕐 Mon–Fri 9–5, Sat 9–4

Edams Museum
✉ Damplein 8
☎ 0299/372 644
🕐 Apr–Oct Tue–Sat
10–4:30, Sun 1:30–4:30
💶 Inexpensive

🛈 Markt 27 ☎ 0900/468
3288 🕐 Mon–Sat 9–5

Stadhuis
✉ Markt
☎ 0182/588 758
🕐 Mon–Fri 10–12, 2–4
💶 Inexpensive

Waag
✉ Markt 35–6
☎ 0182/529 996
🕐 Apr–Oct Tue, Wed, Fri
1–5, Thu 10–5
💶 Inexpensive

Adrie Moerings Pottenbakkerij & Pijpenmakerij
✉ Peperstraat 76
☎ 0182/512 842
🕐 Mon–Fri 9–5, Sat 11–5
💶 Free

EDAM

Home of the famous round, yellow-skinned cheese (covered in red wax for export), Edam, 15km north of Amsterdam, lies inland along a canal from the IJsselmeer. Visit the **Edams Museum**, in a 1530s merchant's house with a floating cellar, for a look at the town's history. A cheese-making display at the Kaaswaag (Cheese-Weighing House) and the beautifully decorated Trouwzaal (Wedding Room) in the 1737 Stadhuis (Town Hall) are worth seeing. The tilting 15th-century Speeltoren (Carillon Tower) has a carillon from 1561. You can tour nearby cheese-making farms; leaflets are available from the VVV office.

GOUDA

Gouda, renowned for its yellow-skinned, cylindrical cheese and clay pipes, is 37km south of Amsterdam. Its striking 15th-century Gothic **Stadhuis** (Town Hall), has a carillon whose chimes are accompanied by figures representing Count Floris V signing the town's charter in 1272. You can learn the story of Gouda and cheese at the Cheese Exhibition in the **Waag** (Weigh-House), and of Gouda and pipes at the **Adrie Moerings Pottenbakkerij & Pijpenmakerij.** Visit the 16th-century Sint-Janskerk to see its superb stained-glass windows, some dating from the 1550s. There's a popular cheese market on Thursday mornings in the Markt from June until August.

DEN HAAG & SCHEVENINGEN ✪✪✪

The Netherlands' administrative capital, The Hague (63km southwest of Amsterdam), and its seaside resort Scheveningen have reached out and touched each other over the years, and it makes sense to visit them together.

Den Haag makes an interesting comparison with Amsterdam, having almost no canals, and being focused on government, the royal court, diplomacy and its role as seat of the International Court of Justice. There's plenty to see, beginning with the Dutch parliament, the Binnenhof, where both chambers of the States General meet and, in its courtyard, the 13th-century Ridderzaal (Hall of the Knights), where the monarch presides over the annual state opening of parliament. You can visit Paleis Lange Voorhout, view Huis ten Bosch (home of Queen Beatrix) from its surrounding park and look at Paleis Noordeinde from the street. For Dutch and international art, including masterpieces by Rembrandt, Vermeer and Van Gogh, visit the Mauritshuis and Haags Gemeentemuseum (Hague Municipal Museum). For variety there's the Omniversum Imax projection theatre; Madurodam, a miniature village, with the best of Holland at a scale of 1:25; and Panorama Mesdag, a panoramic painting of Scheveningen made in 1880–1.

Compared with Zandvoort (➤ 89), Amsterdam's seaside resort, Scheveningen is the height of sophistication. Though it can be a little ragged around the edges, it's well worth the short tram ride from The Hague to visit its superb belle époque beach hotel, the Steigenberger Kurhaus, casino, fancy shops, good seafood and international restaurants, splendid pier and beach. On the last Saturday in May the harbour is the setting for Vlaggetjesdag (Flag Day), when fishing boats compete for the honour of catching the new season's first herring for the Queen.

Peering across at Scheveningen from the resort's magnificent pier

---

🛈 Koningin Julianaplein
☎ 0900/340 3505 🅒
Mon–Fri 8:30–5:30, Sat 10–5, Sun (Jul–Aug) 11–3

Binnenhof/Ridderzaal
✉ Binnenhof 8a
☎ 070/364 6144
🕐 Guided tours Mon–Sat 10–4 (last tour 3:45). Closed pub hols, special events 👤 Moderate

Paleis Lange Voorhout
✉ Lange Voorhout 74
☎ 070/362 4061
🕐 Tue–Sun 11–5
👤 Moderate

Mauritshuis
✉ Korte Vijverberg 8
☎ 070/302 3435
🕐 Tue–Sat 10–5, Sun & pub hols 11–5. Closed 1 Jan, 25 Dec
👤 Expensive

Haags Gemeentemuseum
✉ Stadhouderslaan 41
☎ 070/338 1111
🕐 Tue–Sun and pub hols 11–5 👤 Expensive

Omniversum
✉ President Kennedylaan 5
☎ 0900/666 4837
🕐 Tue–Wed 11–6, Thu–Sun and during hols 11–11. Closed 1 Jan, 25 Dec
👤 Very expensive

Madurodam
✉ George Maduroplein 1
☎ 070/355 3900
🕐 Jul–Aug daily 9–10; Sep–late Mar daily 9–6; late Mar–Jun daily 9–10
👤 Very expensive

Panorama Mesdag
✉ Zeestraat 65
☎ 070/364 4544
🕐 Mon–Sat 10–5, Sun & pub hols 12–5. Closed 25 Dec
👤 Moderate

The splendours of St Bavo's Church are its marvellous organ (far right), and the ornate spire (right)

ℹ️ Stationsplein 1 ☎ 0900/616 1600 🕐 Mon–Fri 9:30–5:30, Sat 10–2

Sint-Bavokerk

✉️ Oude Groenmarkt 23
☎️ 023/532 4399
🕐 Mon–Sat 10–4
✋ Inexpensive

Frans Halsmuseum

✉️ Groot Heiligland 62
☎️ 023/511 5775
🕐 Mon–Sat 11–5, Sun & pub hols 12–5. Closed 1 Jan, 25 Dec
✋ Moderate

HAARLEM ✪✪✪

Just 20km west of Amsterdam, this city of 150,000 is often considered to be the capital's fair little sister, with almost as much canal-fringed, Golden Age allure and far fewer everyday vexations. Founded in the 10th century, Haarlem was the seat of the medieval Counts of Holland and is today North Holland's provincial capital. Its lowest ebb was a seven-month siege (1572–3) during Holland's revolt against Spain when, despite desperate resistance, the Duke of Alva's troops captured the city and massacred half its 40,000 inhabitants.

Haarlem's Grote Markt is dominated by the 80m-high tower, adorned with gilt spheres, of the late-Gothic **Sint-Bavokerk** (built 1370–1520), also known as the Grote Kerk (Great Church). In the bright and richly ornamented interior is a 1738 Christian Müller organ, with more than 5,000 pipes, that was once played by Mozart and Handel. You can see, still embedded in the wall, a cannonball that flew through a window during the Spanish siege. The painter Frans Hals (c1580–1666), who was born in Antwerp and lived and worked in Haarlem for most of his life, is buried in the choir. In addition to such highly individualistic works as *The Gypsy Girl* and *The Laughing Cavalier*, Hals painted group portraits of the *schutters* (musketeers), local militia companies. You can see eight such works, among others, at the **Frans Hals Museum**, including the lively *Banquet of the Officers of the St Hadrian Militia Company* (1627). The museum is in the former Oudemannenhuis, an old men's hospice from 1608.

HOORN ✪✪

This once important seaport is on the IJsselmeer shore, 32km north of the capital. It makes a possible day trip by bike, returning by train. The best place to appreciate Hoorn's maritime past, which has left the town many old sailors' houses and gabled merchants' villas, is at the busy inner harbour, the Binnenhaven, with its 1532 tower, the Hoofdtoren. Visit the **Westfries Museum** in a baroque building dating from 1632 to sample Hoorn's heritage.

LEIDEN ✪✪

Rembrandt's birthplace and the Pilgrim Fathers' refuge before they sailed to America, Leiden is a renowned university town, 36km southwest of Amsterdam. In 1594, botanist Carolus Clusius grew the first tulips in Holland at the botanical garden here. Each year, between 1 and 3 October, Leiden celebrates the raising of the 1574 Spanish siege, when the Dutch Navy sailed across flooded fields after the dikes had been broken, and surprised the Spanish at their dinner of stew.

 Veemarkt 4 ☎ 0900/403 1055 🕐 Mon–Fri 9–5, Sat 9–4

Westfries Museum
✉ Rode Steen 1
☎ 0229/280 028
🕐 Apr–Sep Mon–Fri 11–5, Sat–Sun 2–5. Closed 1 Jan, 30 Apr, 3rd Mon in Aug, 25 Dec

📍 Stationsplein 210
☎ 0900/222 2333
🕐 Mon–Fri 9:30–5:30, Sat 10–2

DID YOU KNOW?

In 1616, Willem Schouten was the first seaman to sail round the southern tip of South America, through the Straits of Magellan, and into the Pacific. He named the rocky, storm-swept point of Tierra del Fuego island Kap Hoorn (Cape Horn) after his home town.

The IJsselmeer's Western Shore

Distance
160km

Time
A day

Start/end point
Amsterdam

Lunch
De Hoofdtoren, Hoorn (➤ 99)

For centuries the Zuiderzee, a stormy North Sea inlet, presented a clear and present danger to low-lying Amsterdam – so the Dutch got rid of it. In 1932, the 30km-long Afsluitdijk (Enclosing Dike) shut out the sea. In its place is the IJsselmeer, a freshwater lake and a wonderful setting for a drive through historic towns and typical Dutch scenery.

Take the A10 Amsterdam ring road east to junction 114 and follow the signs to the lake at Durgerdam. Stay on the lakeside road, heading north.

A causeway leads to Marken (➤ 88), which was once an island. Explore the pretty harbourside village on foot. You can also walk 2km to a lighthouse at the island's tip.

Re-cross the causeway and continue north on the lakeside road.

Monnickendam harbour (➤ 88) is worth visiting, though most people pass through to Volendam (➤ 88), a fishing village where you can have your picture taken wearing traditional Dutch costume. A brief detour through Edam (➤ 80) returns you to the lake.

Continue north through Warder and Scharwoude.

Take a tour around Hoorn (➤ 83), an historic seaport and fishing village.

Hoorn harbour recalls the town's celebrated maritime history

Going east and north along the shore brings you to Enkhuizen.

Visit Enkhuizen's Zuiderzeemuseum by boat. Many fields around the town are awash with tulips in spring.

Continue to Medemblik.

Visit the harbour, the steam train museum and 13th-century Kasteel Radboud (Radboud Castle).

Continue to the Afsluitdijk. Cross over to the Friesland shore or return to Amsterdam on the A7 (E22).

LOOSDRECHTSE PLASSEN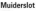

Old peat diggings filled with water form a cluster of lakes, covering more than 2,500 hectares, that have become a popular watersports zone some 20km southeast of Amsterdam. The lakes, some still connected by strips of peaty soil, are surrounded by picturesque villages: Oud-Loosdrecht, Loenen aan de Vecht, and Breukelen, which in the 17th century gave its name to New York's borough of Brooklyn – there's even a tiny Breukelen Bridge over the River Vecht. These once bucolic villages have become busy harbours for pleasure craft and centres for cafés and restaurants, many with waterside terraces.

Fairytale Muiderslot has been beautifully restored inside and out

MUIDEN

The main reason for visiting this IJsselmeer harbour town, 13km east of Amsterdam, handsome though it is, is to see Muiderslot, a turreted, moated castle beside the River Vecht. In 1296, Count Gijsbrecht IV van Aemstel imprisoned and murdered Count Floris V of Holland here. More than three centuries later, the poet Pieter Cornelisz Hooft, a castle steward, founded a literary circle called the Muiderkring (Muiden Circle), which included such luminaries as Hugo Grotius, Joost van den Vondel and Maria Tesselschade.

Muiderslot
✉ Herengracht 1
☎ 0294/261 325
🕐 Guided tours Apr–Sep
Mon–Fri 10–5, Sat–Sun &
pub hols 1–5 (last tour at
4); Nov–Mar Sat–Sun 1–4
(last tour at 3)
💶 Moderate

NAARDEN

This star-shaped, fortified town, 19km east of Amsterdam, was part of a ring of 17th-century defensive works built to protect heavily populated western Holland. Ironically, the town had been sacked earlier by the Spanish. Its Turfpoort (Peat Gateway) Bastion is an appropriate location for the Nederlands Vestingsmuseum (Dutch Fortifications Museum), where you can clamber around the walls and view military exhibits, including weaponry and photographs in the casemates.

**Nederlands
Vestingsmuseum**
✉ Westwalstraat 6
☎ 035/694 5459
🕐 Easter–Oct Tue–Fri
10:30–5, Sat–Sun & pub
hols 12–5; mid-Jun to
Aug also Mon 10:30–5;
Nov–Easter 12–4; Sat
before Christmas to mid-
Jan also Sat & pub hols
12–4. Closed 25 & 31 Dec
🚌 Bus 148

OUDERKERK AAN DE AMSTEL

This handsome village on the River Amstel south of Amsterdam was the seat of the 13th-century Count Gijsbrecht II van Aemstel, who founded Amsterdam. Nowadays there's no doubt which community is in the driving seat. Amsterdammers flock to Ouderkerk to relax in its riverside cafés and restaurants, and it's a popular target for easy cycling excursions along the river.

85

Coolsingel 67 ☎
0900/403 4065 🕒
Mon–Thu 9:30–6, Fri
9:30–9, Sat 9:30–5, Sun
(Apr–Sep) 12–5

Kijkkubussen

✉ Overblaak 70
☎ 010/414 2285
🕒 Jan–Feb Fri–Sun 11–5;
Mar–Dec daily 11–5
👋 Inexpensive

Kunsthal

✉ Museumpark,
Westzeedijk 341
☎ 010/440 0301
🕒 Tue–Sat 10–5, Sun & pub
hols 11–5. Closed 1 Jan,
30 Apr, 25 Dec
👋 Moderate

**Museum Boijmans Van
Beuningen**

✉ Museumpark 18–20
☎ 010/441 9400
🕒 See Kunsthal above
👋 Moderate

Above: *cube houses
overlooking Oude Haven*

ROTTERDAM ✪✪

Rotterdam, birthplace of the humanist Desiderius Erasmus (1466–1536), began developing as a harbour at the end of the 14th century alongside the foreport of Delft (► 79), though it was not until 1886 that it swallowed up Delfshaven. 'Rotterdammers,' say the Dutch, 'are born with their sleeves already rolled up.' That helps explain the speed with which they rebuilt their city, 60km southwest of Amsterdam, which was almost totally destroyed during World War II, and made it the world's most important harbour. The authorities decided in 1945 not to rebuild the devastated city along the old lines, launching instead a bold, controversial and ongoing experiment to create a city of the future. Rotterdam has had all the latest trends in architecture and town planning showered on it and shows no sign of wearying in the quest for modernity. If you like modern architecture, visit the **Kijkkubussen**, one of a group of upended cube-shaped houses on concrete stalks; an apartment tower-block in the shape of a pencil; and an apartment block whose shape has earned it the nickname 'Paper-Clip'.

Grouped conveniently in the Museumpark are the **Kunsthal (Art Hall)**, which mounts art and design exhibitions; **Museum Boijmans Van Beuningen**, whose art collection ranges from Old Masters to the day before yesterday; and the Netherlands Architecture Institute, an appropriate asset for such an architecture-fixated city, though not all of its displays cover modern schools. Get away from museums at Blijdorp Zoo, soar above the harbour at the 188m-high Euromast tower, and tour it on a Spido harbour tour boat.

At Kinderdijk, 12km east of the city, you have the beautiful sight of 19 windmills together in a cluster. These were in use until 1950 to drain the Alblasserwaard polders and are now a popular tourist attraction.

Texel's sandy beaches are as much an attraction as the abundant birdlife

TEXEL ⭐⭐

Texel island, which lies off the North Holland peninsula 70km northwest of Amsterdam, is reached by a 20-minute car ferry crossing from Den Helder, at the tip of the peninsula. Biggest of Holland's Wadden Islands, Texel has a population of 14,000 that surges in summer when visitors pour in for its beaches, boating, cycling and bird-watching. Around 400 bird species have been spotted, including 100 breeding species. You can observe birds at several nature reserves, tour nature trails through dunes and woods, and get close to nature in general, and the island's seal population in particular, on guided tours.

🛈 Emmalaan 66, Den Burg
☎ 0222/312 847
🕐 Mon–Fri 9–6, Sat 9–5

Car ferry
☎ 0222/369 600
🕐 Hourly sailings Mon–Sat 6:35AM–9:35PM, Sun and pub hols 8:35AM to 9:35PM; last return 9:05PM. No reservations

UTRECHT ⭐⭐

Utrecht traces its history back to Roman times and has many memorials of its medieval role as an ecclesiastical centre. About 34km southeast of Amsterdam, the city has a split personality, divided between its old centre along tree-lined Oudegracht and Nieuwegracht – canals whose former warehouses have been turned into cafés and restaurants – and a modern face focused on the vast Hoog Catherijne shopping mall and Vredenburg entertainment complex. Utrecht is dominated by the 14th-century Gothic **Domtoren**, 112m high, and adjacent **Domkerk** (1254–1517), which stands on the site of a cathedral destroyed by a hurricane in 1647.

🛈 Vinkenburgstraat 19
☎ 0900/414 1414
🕐 Mon–Fri 9–6, Sat 9–5

Domtoren and Domkerk
✉ Domplein
☎ Tower: 030/233 3036, cathedral: 030/231 0403
🕐 Cathedral: May–Sep daily 10–5; Oct–Apr Mon–Fri 10–4, Sat 11–3:30, Sun 2–4
💶 Tower: moderate, cathedral: free

87

ℹ️ Zeestraat 37, Volendam
☎ 0299/363 747
🕐 Apr–Oct, daily 10–5;
Nov–Mar, Mon–Sat 10–3

ℹ️ De Zarken 2,
Monnickendam
☎ 0299/651 998
🕐 Mon–Fri 9–5, Sat 9–4

VOLENDAM AND MARKEN ✪✪✪

These two IJsselmeer resorts, 18km and 16km northeast of Amsterdam respectively, are popular with day-trippers by car, bus, bike and guided tour. Long-time rivals, they face each other across just 3km of water, presenting different faces.

Volendam, on the mainland, is Catholic, rambunctious and open; Marken, a former island connected to the mainland by causeway in 1957, is Calvinist, tranquil and insular. In each, some local people can occasionally be seen wearing traditional costume, you're not guaranteed to see this, but you might. You can easily combine the two resorts in one trip, thereby having a chance to compare and contrast.

Volendam's focus is a long, dike-top street along the harbour, lined with souvenir shops, cafés, restaurants and fish-stalls – try the smoked IJsselmeer *paling* (eel), a speciality. Marken has a harbour too, though a smaller one, lined with green-painted wooden houses on stilts, some of which you can visit; others have been turned into cafés. There are tiny hamlets scattered across the former island's polders, and a lighthouse on the shore. From mid-March to October, a tour boat connects the two resorts, sailing from half-hourly to hourly on a half-hour crossing.

The popular face of Dutch tourism on show in Volendam

Between the two resorts – neutral territory, if you like – lies **Monnickendam**, which has its own busy harbour lined with cafés and restaurants, and which makes less fuss than its neighbours over its status as a tourist attraction.

✉️ Zaandam
☎ 075/616 8218
🕐 Apr–Sep, daily 8:30–7:30;
Oct–Mar, daily 9–5
💶 Free to moderate

DE ZAANSE SCHANS ✪✪

This living village and museum, 13km northwest of Amsterdam, offers a glimpse of Dutch life in times past.

Zaanse Schans – bringing the past to life

Set up in 1960 with relocated, green-painted Zaanstreek houses and five windmills, it's almost kitsch, but not quite, thanks to a scenic setting on the River Zaan and the intrinsic interest of the trades it preserves. You can shop at an 18th-century grocery store, and visit a traditional clog-maker, a cheese-maker, pewter workshop, bakery museum, clock museum, working windmills making oil, paint and classic Zaanse mustard, and a sawmill.

ZANDVOORT ✪✪✪

Amsterdam's seaside resort, 25km west of the city, is brash and brassy when it claims its place in the sun every summer (even when there is no sun), and sinks into winter melancholy come the middle of October. Whatever the season or weather, Amsterdammers like nothing better than taking the train here, walking up and down on the beach for an hour or two taking in the atmosphere, then retiring to a café. Zandvoort's long stretch of smooth sand is lined in summer with 40 café-restaurants. You can feel overdressed here wearing only a bikini bottom or swimshorts, particularly at the nudist and gay sections of the beach. Windsurfers are well catered for, and swimming is safe, though the North Sea is generally far from warm.

Away from the beach, splash out in a different way at **Holland Casino Zandvoort**, or catch a motor or motor-cycle race at Circuit Park Zandvoort. For a more leisurely experience, tour the Kennemerduinen National Park's extensive dunes.

🛈 Schoolplein 1 ☎ 023/571 7947 🕐 Apr to mid-Jul & mid-Aug to Sep Mon–Sat 9–5; mid-Jul to mid-Aug Mon–Sat 9–7; Oct–Mar Mon–Sat 10–12:30, 1:30–4:30

Holland Casino Zandvoort
✉ Badhuisplein 7
☎ 023/574 0574
🕐 Daily 1:30PM–2AM
💰 Moderate (passport and 'correct' attire needed)

On the beach at Zandvoort

The North Sea Coast

Distance
145km

Time
A day

Start/end point
Amsterdam

Lunch
De Pêcherie Haarlem aan Zee
(➤ 99)

VVV Castricum
✉ Dorpsstraat 62
☎ 0251/652 009
🕐 Mon 12–5, Tue–Fri
9:30–5, Sat 9:30–2

The coast west of Amsterdam plays host to a constellation of beach resorts, each with its own distinct character. Driving between them and soaking up bracing sea air makes a nice change from wall-to-wall canals and polders.

Take the A8 northwest from Amsterdam to its end, then via a dogleg on the N246 and N203, to the A9 and continue north to Alkmaar. Change to the N9 for Bergen, then west to Bergen aan Zee.

Visit the beach, its dunes, and the Zee Aquarium.

Go south on the coast road through the Duinreservaat (Dune Reserve) to Egmond, then west to Egmond aan Zee.

The resort has a superb beach, a lighthouse and walking trails through the dunes.

Go south to Castricum, then west through the Noordhollands-Castricum Duinreservaat to Castricum aan Zee.

Dune trails, for which you need a pass from VVV Castricum, are particularly good here.

Stop for a walk through the dune landscape at Kennemer

Go south to Beverwijk, then west to Wijk aan Zee.

Near the mouth of the Noordzeekanaal, this resort is too close for comfort to industrial IJmuiden, but its forested dunes zone is attractive.

Go south under the Noordzeekanaal, past IJmuiden, to Haarlem. Take the N208 to Bloemendaal aan Zee.

This little resort adjoins Zandvoort (➤ 89), Amsterdam's main seaside resort. The Kennemerduinen National Park behind the seafront is a great place for hiking.

Return to Amsterdam on the A5/N5 via Haarlem.

Where To...

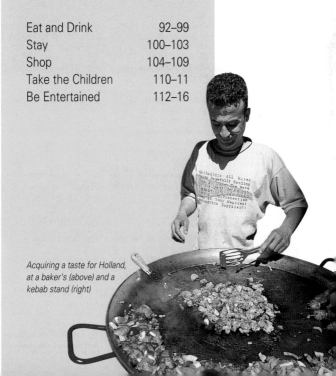

Acquiring a taste for Holland, at a baker's (above) and a kebab stand (right)

Amsterdam

Price Guide

Approximate price per person for a three-course meal, without drinks, but including value-added tax (BTW) and 15 per cent service charge:

€ = under €25
€€ = €25–50
€€€ = over €50

In most restaurants you pay substantially less by ordering the *dagschotel* (dish of the day) or *dagmenu* (menu of the day); some also offer a tourist menu, either in addition to the *dagmenu* or instead of it. Reservations are advised for expensive restaurants. Some others listed here in lower price categories also need to be reserved; because they are so popular they almost never have a free table or they don't have many tables in the first place (or both). In any case it is usually a good idea to phone and check on seat availability. In keeping with Amsterdam's laid-back style, casual dress is acceptable even in the most expensive restaurants – though smart-but-casual will go down better at high-end establishments.

NOTE: All bus/tram numbers relate to trams, unless otherwise stated

Akbar (€€)

Akbar's consistently good curries, tandoori and other dishes don't let Indian cuisine down in this area of abundant but unexceptional international restaurants.

✉ **Korte Leisedwarsstraat 15**
☎ **624 2211** 🕐 **Daily, dinner**
🚊 **1, 2, 5, 6, 7, 10, 20**

Al's Plaice (€)

Never mind the painful pun, Al's traditional British fish 'n' chips are exactly that.

✉ **Nieuwendijk 10** ☎ **427 4192** 🕐 **Mon 5PM–10PM, Wed–Sun noon–10PM** 🚊 **1, 2, 5, 13, 17, 20**

Amsterdam (€€)

A renovated 19th-century water-pumping station is the scene for a cool restaurant, whose menu is a deluge of continental dishes.

✉ **Watertorenplein 6** ☎ **682 2666** 🕐 **Daily 11:30AM–1AM**
🚊 **10**

Asian Caribbean (€–€€)

Big, plant-strewn and bewildering, with cuisine from different Asian countries and Caribbean islands – plus an Argentinian steak house.

✉ **Warmoesstraat 170** ☎ **627 1545** 🕐 **Daily dinner** 🚊 **4, 9, 16, 20, 24, 25**

De Belhamel (€€)

Art nouveau décor and classical music set the tone for polished continental cuisine, and game in season, in an intimate setting with a superb canal view.

✉ **Brouwersgracht 60** ☎ **622 1095** 🕐 **Daily dinner** 🚊 **18, 22**

Bodega Keyser (€€)

Old Amsterdam favourite beside the Concertgebouw,

specialising in seafood and traditional Dutch dishes. Popular with concert-goers.

✉ **Van Baerlestraat 96**
☎ **671 1441** 🕐 **Mon–Sat 9AM–midnight, Sun 11AM–midnight** 🚊 **2, 3, 5, 12, 16, 20**

Bolhoed (€–€€)

Two candlelit canalside rooms enlivened with ethnic art, and hard to beat for the adventurous vegetarian recipes prepared and served with light-hearted panache.

✉ **Prinsengracht 60–62**
☎ **626 1803** 🕐 **Daily noon–11 (Sat 11–11AM)** 🚊 **13, 14, 17, 20**

Bordewijk (€€–€€€)

Deft Mediterranean and Asian culinary touches combine with minimalist décor, adding a modern slant to French dining at this well regarded Jordaan restaurant.

✉ **Noordermarkt 7** ☎ **624 3899** 🕐 **Tue–Sun dinner**
🚊 **Bus 18, 22**

De Brakke Grond (€–€€)

Flemish Cultural Centre's darkly atmospheric restaurant, serving bountiful portions of Belgian food, including *waterzooi* (chicken or fish stew) and *paling* (eel), along with better-known steak-frites and mussels. You can wash them down with great beers.

✉ **Nes 43** ☎ **626 0044**
🕐 **Tue–Sat noon–11**
🚊 **4, 9, 14, 16, 20, 24, 25**

Brasserie De Poort (€€)

Wooden beams and Delft blue tiles in an 1870 tavern are the backdrop for fine Dutch dining. Every thousandth steak comes with a free bottle of wine.

✉ **Hotel Die Port van Cleve, Nieuwezijds Voorburgwal**

176–180 ☎ 624 0047
🌐 Mon–Fri 7AM–10:30AM and 6–10:30PM, Sat–Sun 6–10:30AM and noon–10:30PM 🚊 1, 2, 5, 13, 14, 17, 20

Brasserie Schiller (€€)
Restored, century-old *jugendstil* monument, rich in wood-panelling and etched and stained glass, serving classic Dutch and international cuisine.
✉ Hotel Schiller, Rembrandtplein 26–36 ☎ 554 0700 🌐 Daily 7AM–11PM 🚊 4, 9, 14, 20

Breitner (€€)
Carefully prepared French dishes in a light and airy setting with a fine view over the Amstel.
✉ Amstel 212 ☎ 627 7879 🌐 Daily 5PM–midnight 🚊 4, 9, 14, 20

Café Américain (€€)
Popularity with tourists has slightly dimmed the modish cachet of this resplendent art deco café, but the fancy continental cuisine remains effective.
✉ American Hotel, Leidsekade 97 ☎ 556 3232 🌐 Daily 10:30AM–midnight 🚊 1, 2, 5, 6, 7, 10, 20

Café Roux (€€)
French cuisine in an elegant art nouveau setting that used to be the old town hall's canteen. A Karel Appel mural, *Inquisitive Children* (1949), is a proud fixture.
✉ Grand Westin Demeure Hotel, Oudezijds Voorburgwal 197 ☎ 555 3560 🌐 Daily noon–6 🚊 4, 9, 14, 16, 20, 24, 25

Christophe (€€€)
Chef Jean Christophe combines French sensibility with a dash of American seasoning to good effect in his chic canalside restaurant.
✉ Leliegracht 46 ☎ 625 0807 🌐 Dinner only Tue–Sat 🚊 13, 14, 17, 20

Duende (€)
Dark, bustling *tapas* café, popular with Spanish expats. with a large choice of *tapas* – hot and cold snacks.
✉ Lindengracht 62 ☎ 420 6692 🌐 Daily 5PM–1AM 🚍 Bus 18, 20

Espresso Corner Baton (€)
Good for a quick, light lunch, this bustling place serves salads, sandwiches, quiches and more. In summer a large pavement terrace allows you to enjoy the canalside ambience and watch the tour boats chugging past.
✉ Herengracht 82 ☎ 624 8195 🌐 Mon–Fri 8–6, Sat–Sun 9–6 🚊 1, 2, 5, 13, 17, 20

Excelsior (€€€)
Haunt of celebrities and an occasional royal, this superior restaurant beside the Amstel matches top-flight Continental cuisine with plush good looks. Consider the fixed-price menus for affordable dining. Unusually for Amsterdam, but understandably, formal attire is required.
✉ Hôtel de l'Europe, Nieuwe Doelenstraat 2–8 ☎ 531 1777 🌐 Daily 7–11, 12:30–2:30 (except Sat), 7–10:30 🚊 4, 9, 14, 20, 24, 25

De Falafel Koning (€)
You won't find better Israeli falafel than at this snackbar opposite the Tuschinski cinema.
✉ Regulierssteeg 2 ☎ 421 1423 🌐 Daily 10AM –1AM 🚊 4, 9, 14, 20

Gare de l'Est (€€)
Moody, former working-class coffee-house, enhanced by a conservatory, serving a set, daily-changing Mediterra-nean menu, with the emphasis on French dishes.
✉ Cruquiusweg 9 ☎ 463 0620 🌐 Daily 6PM–1 or 2AM 🚍 Bus 39, 59

Tipping
You don't need to worry too much about this in most Dutch restaurants. As service is usually included in the bill, locals tend to leave minimal tips, if any at all, and although the staff have no objection to receiving tips they won't pursue you for them. If you want to leave a Dutch-style tip, in a cheap to moderately priced place, round the bill up to a euro or two; in an expensive place take it up to the nearest five euros. You may want to leave more if you have had particularly good service, if there are more than four people in your group, or if you are dining in a very expensive restaurant.

Where to Eat

If you are on a budget or are set on a truly Dutch experience, try an *eetcafé*. In these café-restaurants the food runs the gamut from traditional Dutch, to modern, stylish, even experimental cooking, though generally not in the same place, and usually for significantly less than you pay in a full-blown restaurant.

'Coffee shops' are not there to sell coffee – although their coffee is often surprisingly good – but legally tolerated soft drugs. You buy coffee in a café and occasionally in a *koffiehuis*. Your nose will quickly tell you the difference if it catches a whiff of the bitter-smelling fug that passes for an atmosphere in a 'coffee shop'.

Gary's Muffins and Bagels (€)

Enter a world of bagels, muffins and cheesecake at this breezy American snack bar. You can choose from eight different kinds of bagel, and 20 different toppings.

📫 Reguliersdwarsstraat 53
☎ 420 2406 🕐 Daily noon–3 or 4AM 🚊 4, 9, 14, 16, 20, 24, 25

Girassol (€)

The oldest and best Portuguese restaurant in town, with a menu that covers the mainland and includes dishes from Madeira and the Azores.

📫 Weesperzijde 135
☎ 692 3471 🕐 Daily dinner
🚊 6, 7, 10

Greenwoods (€)

Homey English tea room, serving home-made scones, with jam and clotted cream, chocolate cake and lemon meringue pie.

📫 Singel 103 ☎ 623 7071
🕐 Daily 9:30–7 🚊 1, 2, 5, 13, 17, 20

Haesje Claes (€–€€)

Eight wood-beamed dining rooms in a house from 1520, serving traditional Dutch cuisine with a 'from canapés to caviar' ethos.

📫 Spuistraat 273–5 ☎ 624 9998 🕐 Daily noon–midnight
🚊 1, 2, 5

Hemelse Modder (€€)

Chocoholics will appreciate the chocolate mousse that gives 'Heavenly Mud' its name. But first sample a vegetarian main course.

📫 Oude Waal 9–11 ☎ 624 3203 🕐 Dinner only Tue–Sun
🚇 Nieuwmarkt

De Jaren (€–€€)

Trendy grand café in a vast, remodelled bank, serving drinks and snacks downstairs and Dutch and continental food upstairs. The Amstel waterfront terrace is a big draw.

📫 Nieuwe Doelenstraat 20–22
☎ 625 5771 🕐 Sun–Thu 10AM–1AM, Fri–Sat 10AM–2AM
🚊 4, 9, 16, 20, 24, 25

Kantjil en de Tijger (€€)

'Antelope and the Tiger' spurns the colonial look and serves spicy Javanese food in a cool, modern setting.

📫 Spuistraat 291–3 ☎ 620 0994 🕐 Daily dinner 🚊 1, 2, 5

De Kas (€€)

Opened in 2001, this out-of-the-way eatery in a 1926 greenhouse quickly became *the* place for trendy locals. The international dishes with a Mediterranean slant are from a couple of variations on a 3-course, daily-changing fixed menu.

📫 Kamerlingh Onneslaan 3
☎ 462 4562 🕐 Mon–Fri 12–3, 6:30–10, Sat 6:30–10 🚊 9

't Klein Kalfje (€)

Old-fashioned Dutch café-restaurant on the edge of town. It attracts an office-worker crowd in summer for lunch on its sheltered, riverside terrace.

📫 Amsteldijk 355 ☎ 644 5338 🕐 Sun–Fri 10AM–10PM (8PM in winter) 🚊 Bus 148

De Knijp (€€)

Instead of gulping down dinner then dashing off to the Concertgebouw, dine here after the concert on French and Dutch dishes served in a split-level bistro.

📫 Van Baerlestraat 134
☎ 671 4248 🕐 Mon–Fri noon–3; daily 5:30PM–1:30AM
🚊 3, 5, 12, 16, 20, 24

Het Land van Walem (€€)

Set aside the latest interior design and an urbane menu, and you may find the two terraces – one outside beside the canal, the other in a garden at the back – to be its chief selling point.

📫 Keizersgracht 449

☎ 625 3544 ⊙ Sun–Thu
9AM–1AM; Fri–Sat 9AM–2AM
🚊 1, 2, 5

Lovers (€€€)
A candlelit dinner while
cruising on the canals,
watching the city's historic
gables glide past, is almost
guaranteed to be a romantic
experience.
✉ Prins Hendrikkade (at
Centraal Station) ☎ 622 2181
⊙ Apr–Oct daily 7:30PM; Nov–
Mar Wed, Fri, Sat 7:30PM 🚊 1,
2, 4, 5, 9, 13, 16, 17, 20, 24, 25

Luxembourg (€)
Grand café with a power-
user image, where the club
sandwiches are renowned
and the dim sum and other
snacks derive from top city
restaurants.
✉ Spuistraat 22–24 ☎ 620
6264 ⊙ Sun–Fri 9AM–1AM,
Fri–Sat 9AM–2AM 🚊 1, 2, 5

Mangerie de Kersentuin
(€€–€€€)
Informal yet polished, with
dishes from around the
world adapted to mostly
Dutch ingredients,
distinctively prepared.
✉ Bilderberg Garden Hotel,
Dijsselhofplantsoen 7 ☎ 570
5600 ⊙ Mon–Fri lunch,
Mon–Sat dinner 🚊 5, 16, 24

Memories of India (€€)
Delicately flavoured tandoori,
Moghlai and vegetarian
cuisine in a setting that
adopts a restrained version
of Indian décor.
✉ Reguliersdwarsstraat 88
☎ 623 5710 ⊙ Daily dinner
🚊 4, 9, 14, 20

Metz (€)
The panoramic canal views
from this comfortably
English sixth-floor café
distract memorably from
afternoon tea, as does the
1933 round glass rooftop
designed by Gerrit Rietveld.
✉ Metz & Co, Keizersgracht
455/Leidsestraat 34–6 ☎ 520

7020 ⊙ Mon 11–6, Tue, Wed,
Fri, Sat 9:30–6, Thu 9:30–9. Sun
12–5 🚊 1, 2, 5

Mokkalie (€€)
One of a handful of Korean
restaurants in the city. It
does a particularly fine
bulgogi (marinated beef
grilled at your table), in a
plant-strewn setting to the
chirping of exotic birds.
✉ Utrechtsestraat 42 ☎ 625
9251 ⊙ Dinner only. Closed
Mon 🚊 4

Morita-Ya (€)
Traditional Japanese snack
bar that eschews the
hallowed atmosphere of
many Japanese restaurants
in favour of a convivial local
style, and serves great sushi
and sashimi.
✉ Zeedijk 18 ☎ 638 0756
⊙ Dinner Thu– Tue 🚊 1, 2, 4,
5, 9, 13, 16, 17, 20, 24, 25

De Oesterbar (€€–€€€)
The ground floor at this
seafood specialist is smart
but casual; formal elegance
reigns upstairs in the main
dining-room.
✉ Leidseplein 10 ☎ 623 2988
⊙ Daily noon–1AM 🚊 1, 2, 5,
6, 7, 10

Pacifico (€€)
Authentic Mexican food in
a cramped and smoky
bodega, with a wide-ranging
menu, including vegetarian
dishes.
✉ Warmoesstraat 31 ☎ 624
2911 ⊙ Daily dinner 🚊 1, 2,
4, 5, 9, 13, 16, 17, 20, 24, 25

Pasta e Basta (€€)
Very popular partly because
of its chi-chi Italian food and
partly because the staff are
liable to burst into live opera
at every opportunity.
✉ Nieuwe Spiegelstraat 8
☎ 422 2229 ⊙ Daily
6PM–midnight 🚊 16, 24, 25

Pier 10 (€€)
Choose from a wide-ranging

Misconstrued Spice
When the Dutch began
colonising the Spice
Islands of the East Indies
during the 17th century,
they got more than
seasoning out of them.
They developed a taste for
the exotic local cuisine
that survived Indonesian
independence in 1949 and
has bequeathed Holland
an abundance of
Indonesian restaurants.
Most of them serve
rijsttafel (➤ 53). A myth
has grown up around this
'typically Indonesian' meal
that isn't. Dutch colonists
invented it, constantly
adding more dishes to a
basic Indonesian meal until
the table groaned under
their weight. *Rijsttafel*
makes a great introduction
to this national cuisine,
and a great dining
experience – so much so
that some Chinese, Thai,
Vietnamese and Japanese
restaurants have adopted
the approach.

Al Fresco Dining

Amsterdammers are fresh-air fanatics. At the first hint of good weather, restaurants and cafés with outdoor terraces fill up instantly, while those without – anywhere, on the vine. The city is a terrace-hound's dream. Hundreds spread out tables and chairs in squares such as Leidseplein and Rembrandtplein, along the canals and the River Amstel, beside the harbour, in parks and back gardens, on rooftops, quiet side-streets and busy main streets – anywhere, in fact, where there's space and the prospect of catching some sun.

international menu in a glass-fronted 1930s shipping office with an unbeatable harbour view at the end of a pier behind Centraal Station.
✉ Steiger 10 ☎ 624 8276
🕐 Daily dinner 🚋 1, 2, 4, 5, 9, 13, 16, 17, 20, 24, 25

De Prins (€–€€)

Bustling brown café (▶ 114) with an above-average, small restaurant that fills up fast, and with a daily changing menu of Dutch and vaguely French dishes chalked on blackboards.
✉ Prinsengracht 124 ☎ 624 9382 🕐 Daily 10AM–midnight
🚋 13, 14, 17, 20

La Rive (€€€)

High-end French cuisine with a light, modern touch delivered in a plush and formal two-Michelin-star *salle* overlooking the Amstel.
✉ Amstel Intercontinental Hotel, Professor Tulpplein 1
☎ 622 6060 🕐 Mon–Fri lunch, Mon–Sat dinner. Closed Sat–Sun lunch, Sun dinner
🚋 6, 7, 10, 20

Rose's Cantina (€–€€)

Noisy place whose Tex-Mex food in a vaguely Mexican setting is unexceptional, yet whose camaraderie – and great margaritas – mean it's hard to get a table.
✉ Reguliersdwarsstraat 38–40 ☎ 625 9797 🕐 Daily dinner
🚋 1, 2, 5

Royal Café De Kroon (€€€)

Turn-of-the-century grand café that closed during the 1960s and reopened to general acclaim during the 1990s. You order from an eclectic world menu and can sit in the palm-court interior or on an enclosed balcony overlooking the square.
✉ Rembrandtplein 17 ☎ 625 2011 🕐 Daily 10AM–1AM (Fri–Sat 2AM) 🚋 4, 9, 14, 20

La Ruche (€)

Take the weight off shopping-weary feet over coffee and apple-pie with fresh cream in this department store café overlooking the Dam.
✉ De Bijenkorf, Dam 1 ☎ 621 8080 🕐 Mon–Wed, Sat 9:30–6, Thu 9:30–9, Sun noon–6
🚋 4, 9, 14, 16, 20, 24, 25

Rum Runners (€–€€)

Caribbean food and cocktails are served in a tropical setting in the Westerkerk's former coach house beside the Anne Frankhuis.
✉ Prinsengracht 277 ☎ 627 4079 🕐 Mon–Thu 2PM–1AM, Fri–Sun 2PM–2AM 🚋 13, 14, 17, 20

Sal Meijer's (€)

For the finest kosher snacks and sandwiches in town, head for Amsterdam South and this focal point of the city's Jewish community. Or call and ask about a delivery to your hotel.
✉ Scheldstraat 45 ☎ 673 1313 🕐 Sun–Fri 10–7:30
🚋 25

Sea Palace (€€)

It might not have the best Chinese food in town, but eating aboard a pagoda-style floating restaurant in the harbour, modelled on Hong Kong's famous Jumbo restaurant, adds romance to the experience.
✉ Oosterdokskade 8 ☎ 626 4777 🕐 Daily noon–midnight
🚋 1, 2, 4, 5, 9, 13, 16, 17, 20, 24, 25

Shibli (€€€)

Sit on a sofa inside a tent amid Bedouin ornaments and rugs, dining on a sophisticated Arab banquet, and finish with a puff of apple-and-honey tobacco from a *hookah* (water-pipe).
✉ Hotel Krasnapolsky, Dam 9 ☎ 330 8082 🕐 Thu–Sun dinner 🚋 4, 9, 14, 16, 20, 24, 25

De Silveren Spiegel (€€)

The 'Silver Mirror', in twin step-gabled houses dating from 1614, reflects good taste with sophisticated traditional Dutch cuisine enhanced by a continental tang.

✉ Kattegat 4–6 ☎ 624 6589
🕐 Mon–Sat dinner 🚋 1, 2, 5, 13, 17, 20

't Swarte Schaep (€€)

Dark wooden furniture and oak beams from which hang brass pots filled with flowers are the backdrop for the 'Black Sheep's' traditional Dutch and classic continental cooking.

✉ Korte Leidsedwarsstraat 24 ☎ 622 3021 🕐 Daily noon–11 🚋 1, 2, 5, 6, 7, 10

Tempo Doeloe (€€)

Although served on fine china atop linen tablecloths, a few of the *rijsttafel* dishes here can be as fiery as Krakatoa erupting. Don't let that put you off sampling some of the city's best Indonesian dining.

✉ Utrechtsestraat 75 ☎ 625 6718 🕐 Daily dinner 🚋 4

Traîterie Grekas (€€)

If you can get a seat at this tiny, authentic Greek eatery, most of which's business comes from its takeaway service, grab it. Salad dishes and main courses are on display behind glass; you point to what you want and it's brought to your table.

✉ Singel 311 ☎ 620 3590
🕐 Tue–Fri and Sun 4PM–9:30PM, Sat 1PM–9:30PM 🚋 1, 2,5

Vertigo (€€)

Brown café setting, where menu dishes occasionally reflect themes from the adjacent Film Museum – a Japanese film season might be complemented by sushi and sashimi. The open-air terrace in the park is one of the best in town.

✉ Vondelpark 3 ☎ 612 3021
🕐 Daily 11AM (from 10 during Jul–Aug)–1AM 🚋 1, 2, 3, 5, 6, 12, 20

D'Vijff Vlieghen (€€)

With seven individually decorated dining-rooms, the 'Five Flies' flits through a variety of Old Dutch interior styles while focusing culinary attention on light, sophisticated New Dutch cooking.

✉ Spuistraat 294–302 ☎ 624 8369 🕐 Daily dinner 🚋 1, 2, 5

In de Waag (€€)

The ground floor of an old city gate and weigh house (► 73) has been transformed into a restaurant with a medieval look – you dine at long, candlelit benches – and totally modern taste from a wide range of international dishes.

✉ Nieuwmarkt 4 ☎ 422 7772
🕐 Daily 10AM–1AM
🚇 Nieuwmarkt

Wildschut (€–€€)

A chic, art deco bistro that attracts an arts and media crowd and serves up international dishes from BLTs through pasta to 'surf and turf'. When the sun shines, the curving pavement terrace is one of the best in town.

✉ Roelof Hartplein 1–3 ☎ 676 8220 🕐 Mon–Fri 9AM–1AM, Sat 10:30AM–1AM, Sun 9:30AM–midnight 🚋 3, 5, 12, 20, 24

Le Zinc…et les Dames (€€)

Hearty portions of provincial French cuisine in a wood-beamed canalside warehouse converted to a fashionably homey restaurant.

✉ Prinsengracht 999 ☎ 622 9044 🕐 Tue–Sat dinner only 🚋 4

Vegetarians

The Dutch have traditionally been meat-and-veg people. More often now the meat is left out and the veg dressed up in a variety of internationally minded ways. You will find no shortage of purely vegetarian eateries, many with a style that leaves the scrubbed-pine-and-sandals image light years behind; and many more mixed restaurants now have a special place for vegetarians on their menu. A full vegetarian restaurant listed here is Bolhoed (► 92).

Excursions from the City

Dutch Taste

Look out for soup tureen icons in the red, white and blue colours of the Dutch flag, that identify the 500 or so members of the Neerlands Dis (Netherlands Dish) association. Its restaurants dedicate themselves to preparing the best Dutch produce from land and sea and serving up the results in traditional fashion and to a high standard of quality. There's no better way to go Dutch.

Delft
Spijshuis de Dis (€€)
Steaks are the speciality and Dutch food with a touch of class is the trademark at this traditional restaurant.
✉ Beestenmarkt 36 ☎ 015/213 1782 🕐 Thu–Tue 5PM–9:30PM.

Stads Pannekoekhuys (€)
Traditional pancake house with 90 different kinds of pancake on its roster.
✉ Oude Delft 113–115 ☎ 015/213 0193 🕐 Apr–Sep daily 11–9; Oct–Mar Tue–Sun 11–9

Edam
De Fortuna (€€)
The flower-bedecked canalside terrace and wood-beamed, Old Holland interior are the setting for typically Dutch, with a dash of French, menu dishes.
✉ Spuistraat 1–7 ☎ 0299/371 671 🕐 Daily 10–10

Gouda
Mallemolen (€€)
Canalside restaurant with Old Dutch looks and French cuisine – even the cheeses, in this most emblematic of Dutch cheese towns, are of French provenance.
✉ Oosthaven 72 ☎ 0182/515 430 🕐 Tue–Fri noon–2PM and 5PM–midnight, Sat–Sun 5PM–midnight

Den Haag & Scheveningen
Ducdalf (€€)
Nautical style in a fishing harbour setting. It doesn't make fish a fetish, but provides a large variety with good taste. There are meat dishes, too.
✉ Dr Lelykade 5, Scheveningen ☎ 070/355 7692 🕐 Daily noon–10

't Goude Hooft (€€)
Quaint 17th-century looks disguise the effects of a 20th-century fire. Rebuilt in the old style, with wooden beams and brass chandeliers, it's a great place for everything from a beer to a full-scale Dutch meal, in the handsome interior or on a terrace overlooking the square.
✉ Groenmarkt 13, The Hague ☎ 070/346 9713 🕐 Mon–Sat 10AM–midnight, Sun 11AM–midnight

Greve (€)
A brightly lit café and a cosy restaurant are the two contrasting faces of this fashionable place, with an international menu that emphasises Mediterranean dishes.
✉ Torenstraat 138, The Hague ☎ 070/360 3919 🕐 Cafe: daily 10AM–1AM; restaurant: Sun–Wed 6PM–10PM, Thu–Sat 6PM–11PM

Kandinsky (€€–€€€)
A fine restaurant with a great beachside location and sea view. Serves superior French and Mediterranean cuisine.
✉ Steigenberger Kurhaus Hotel, Gevers Deynootplein 30, Scheveningen ☎ 070/416 2636 🕐 Mon–Fri 12–10 (no lunch Jul–Aug), 6–10:30, Sat 6–10:30

Haarlem
Jacobus Pieck (€–€€)
Stylish café-restaurant with a shady garden terrace and an eclectic menu that runs from snack-type fare at lunchtime to nicely done Dutch and international dishes for dinner.
✉ Warmoesstraat 18 ☎ 023/532 6144 🕐 Mon–Sat 10AM–11PM, Sun noon–11PM

De Pêcherie Haarlem aan Zee (€€)
Bright and breezy seafood specialist, kitted out with beach props and marine fittings, and a menu of well-prepared fish dishes.

✉ Oude Groenmarkt 10 ☎ 023/531 4848 🕐 Mon–Sat noon–midnight, Sun 5PM–midnight

Hoorn
De Hoofdtoren (€–€€)
A stonebuilt harbourside defence tower from 1532 is an atmospheric setting for modest Dutch fare such as steaks and grilled fish.

✉ Hoofd 2 ☎ 0229/215 487 🕐 Daily 10–10

Leiden
Stadscafé Van der Werff (€)
This busy café-restaurant serves a range of European dishes in a characterful 1930s mansion.

✉ Steenstraat 2 ☎ 071/513 0335 🕐 Daily 10:30–10

Rotterdam
Brasserie Henkes (€€)
A former gin distillery with a waterfront terrace and an old-fashioned interior, serving Dutch and European dishes.

✉ Voorhaven 17 ☎ 010/425 5596 🕐 Daily 11:30AM–midnight (kitchen closes at 10)

Old Dutch (€€)
Alongside a raft of tasty, traditional dishes, some equally good French ones add a dash of sophistication.

✉ Rochussenstraat 20 ☎ 010/436 0344 🕐 Mon–Fri noon–midnight, Sat 6PM–midnight

Texel
Hostellerie Keijser (€€)
Texel specialities such as the lamb that grazes on the island's salty grass, and fish, in a homey setting.

✉ Herenstraat 34, Den Hoorn ☎ 0222/319 623 🕐 Daily noon–10

Utrecht
Stadskasteel Oudaen (€€–€€€)
Restaurant and café in a 14th-century canalside house. The menu leans towards Dutch and European dishes, often with a medieval slant.

✉ Oudegracht 99 ☎ 030/231 1864 🕐 Café: daily 10AM–2AM; restaurant: Mon–Sat 5:30PM–10PM

Volendam & Marken
Spaander (€€)
Old Dutch dining room that looks like a sailing ship interior, serving Dutch meals with the stress on seafood.

✉ Spaander Hotel, Haven 15–19, Volendam ☎ 0299/363595 🕐 Daily 10–10

De Taanderij (€)
French and vegetarian dishes predominate at this refined interpretation of a traditional Dutch *eethuis*. The coffee and apple-pie with cream is state of the art.

✉ Havenbuurt 1, Marken ☎ 0299/602 206 🕐 Apr–Sep daily 10–10; Oct–Mar Tue–Sun 10–10, Sun 6–10

Zaanse Schans
De Hoop op d' Swarte Walvis (€€€)
Epicurean bliss on the banks of the River Zaan, with mainly French and Dutch dishes served indoors or on a riverside terrace.

✉ Kalverringdijk 15 ☎ 075/616 5629 🕐 Mon–Sat noon–2:30, 6–10

Zandvoort
't Familie Restaurant (€)
Goes a little beyond standard fare, with French-influenced meat courses and stewed eel for the determinedly Dutch, in a breezy family restaurant.

✉ Kerkstraat 27 ☎ 023/571 2537 🕐 Daily noon–10

Rijsttafel Wars
Amsterdam considers itself Holland's market leader in everything, and it is particularly confident that its line-up of Indonesian restaurants is the best in the land. So too, does The Hague, ably supported by its seaside resort, Scheveningen. Both Amsterdam and The Hague point to their extensive ethnic Indonesian communities and to the authentic nature of their local champions in the genre. It's all a matter of taste, of course, and neither city suffers from a lack of choice. If you want an informed part in the debate, be prepared to undertake extensive, but rewarding, research.

Amsterdam

Hotel Rates

Rates are for double rooms; in some hotels you get a reduction for single occupancy of a double. A 5 per cent city tax is added to rates in 5-star hotels. Most hotels accept credit cards, though some budget hotels may ask you not to use them.
In general, only expensive hotels charge extra for breakfast. 'Breakfast included' can mean anything from an excellent full, buffet, Continental or Dutch breakfast; some budget hotels interpret 'Dutch' breakfast to mean a cup of miserable coffee, an ultra-hard-boiled egg, and a couple of thin, curly slices of cheese and ham.

€ = under €100
€€ = €100–250
€€€ = over €250

NOTE: All bus/tram numbers relate to trams, unless otherwise stated

Acacia (€)

Small Jordaan hotel owned by an enthusiastic couple who keep things comfortable and friendly. Also rooms on a nearby houseboat.
✉ Lindengracht 251 ☎ 622 1460; fax 638 0748;
www.hotelacacia.nl 🚊 3, 10

De Admiraal (€)

A 17th-century spice warehouse with a nautical style makes a romantic setting for a canalside hotel. The rooms don't quite match the cosy public spaces.
✉ Herengracht 563
☎ 626 2150; fax 623 4625
🚊 4, 9, 16, 20

American (€€€)

Fanciful mix of Venetian gothic and *Jugendstil* distinguishes a hotel that's maybe a little too aware of its own good looks. The art nouveau Café Américain is a city landmark (► 93).
✉ Leidsekade 97 ☎ 556 3000; fax 556 3001;
www.amsterdam-american.crowneplaza.com
🚊 1, 2, 5, 6, 7, 10, 20

Amstel Botel (€)

Floating hotel that fits right in with Amsterdam's watery origins. Outboard rooms afford a good view of the old harbour area. Facilities are modern and comfortable.
✉ Oosterdokskade 2–4
☎ 626 4247; fax 639 1952
🚇 Centraal Station 🚊 1, 2, 4, 5, 9, 13, 16, 17, 20, 24, 25

Amsterdam (€€)

Fully modernised behind its 18th-century façade, on one of the city's liveliest streets. De Roode Leeuw restaurant serves excellent traditional Dutch food.
✉ Damrak 93–94 ☎ 555 0666; fax 620 4716;
www.hotelamsterdam.nl
🚇 Centraal Station 🚊 4, 9, 14, 16, 20, 24, 25

Arena (€€)

A converted 19th-century orphanage hosts a youth-oriented hotel with stylish modern rooms and one of the city's hottest dance clubs, and a café-restaurant with a garden terrace.
✉ 's Gravesandestraat 51
☎ 663 3021; fax 663 2649;
www.hotelarena.nl 🚊 3, 7, 10

Belga (€)

Backpackers' *pied-à-terre*, with large rooms suitable for multiple occupancy and a friendly, family-owned style that complements a 17th-century building designed by Rembrandt's frame-maker.
✉ Hartenstraat 8 ☎ 624 9080; fax 623 6862 🚊 1, 2, 5, 13, 17

City Hostel Vondelpark (€)

A big new hostel built around an old one in the city's famous park, adding a range of modern options from doubles and family rooms to small dormitories, some of which are women-only.
✉ Zandpad 5, Vondelpark
☎ 589 8999; fax 589 8955;
www.njhc.org/vondelpark
🚊 1, 2, 5, 20

Estheréa (€€)

Family-owned hotel that's an ideal compromise between modern facilities and traditional Dutch style, with a great location in 17th-century canalside houses, and well-equipped rooms.
✉ Singel 303–9 ☎ 624 5146; fax 623 9001; www.estherea.nl
🚊 1, 2, 5, 20

De l'Europe (€€€)
Prestigious hotel combining turn-of-the-19th-century architecture with opulent fittings and the most modern amenities, in an unbeatable riverside setting.

✉ **Nieuwe Doelenstraat 2–8**
☎ **531 1777; fax 531 1778;**
www.leurope.nl 🚊 **4, 9, 16, 20, 24, 25**

Golden Tulip Barbizon Palace (€€€)
Luxury and modern amenities concealed behind the façades of a row of 17th-century houses facing Centraal Station.

✉ **Prins Hendrikkade 59–72**
☎ **556 4564; fax 624 3353;**
www.goldentuliphotels.nl/
gtbpalace 🚇 **Centraal Station**
🚊 **1, 2, 4, 5, 9, 13, 16, 17, 20, 24, 25**

Grand Hotel Krasnapolsky (€€€)
Built in the 1860s, the 'Kras' has spread through adjacent buildings, and added up-to-the-minute amenities to its venerable core. Highlight is the *belle époque* Wintertuin (Winter Garden) restaurant.

✉ **Dam 9** ☎ **554 8080; fax 622 8607; www.krasnapolsky.nl**
🚊 **4, 9, 14, 16, 20, 24, 25**

Grand Sofitel Demeure (€€€)
During its 400-plus years, this has been a convent, a gentlemen's residence, Admiralty offices and the town hall. It's now a plush hotel with all amenities.

✉ **Oudezijds Voorburgwal 197**
☎ **555 3111; fax 555 3222;**
www.thegrand.nl 🚊 **4, 9, 16, 20, 24, 25**

Bilderberg Hotel Jan Luyken (€€€)
Flawless and personable service in a graceful 19th-century town house on a quiet street near Vondelpark, Museumplein and P C Hooftstraat's shopping.

✉ **Jan Luykenstraat 54–8**
☎ **573 0730; fax 676 3841;**
www.janluyken.nl
🚊 **2, 3, 5, 10, 12**

Die Port van Cleve (€€)
One-time Heineken brewery turned hotel, restored and renovated, with modern yet comfortable rooms.

✉ **Nieuwezijds Voorburgwal 176–80** ☎ **624 4860; fax 622 0240; www.dieportvancleve.com**
🚊 **1, 2, 5, 13, 17, 20**

Pulitzer (€€–€€€)
A real prizewinner, spread through two dozen 17th- and 18th-century canal houses with gardens. Facilities among the bare brick and oak beams are generally modern and stylish.

✉ **Prinsengracht 315–331**
☎ **523 5235; fax 627 6753;**
www.pulitzer.nl
🚊 **13, 14, 17, 20**

Seven Bridges (€€)
Small and exquisite, with a view of seven bridges, individually styled rooms, lots of antiques, and owners who really do treat their guests like family friends.

✉ **Reguliersgracht 31** ☎ **623 1329 (also fax)** 🚊 **16, 24, 25**

Sint-Nicolaas (€)
If a former factory doesn't sound appealing, rest assured that this rambling place near Centraal Station has a touch of class and comfortable facilities.

✉ **Spuistraat 1a** ☎ **626 1384; fax 623 0979** 🚇 **Centraal Station** 🚊 **1, 2, 5, 13, 17, 20**

Van Ostade Bicycle Hotel (€)
Small, well-kept place that hires bicycles and gives maps and advice on how to discover the city's less well-known places by bike.

✉ **Van Ostadestraat 123**
☎ **679 3452; fax 671 5213;**
www.bicyclehotel.com
🚊 **3, 12, 20, 24, 25**

Hotel Tips
Two-fifths of Amsterdam's 30,000 hotel beds are in 4- and 5-star properties, which can make things difficult for people wanting mid-range and budget accommodation, particularly at peak times such as during the spring tulip season and summer. It's always best to book ahead.

If you arrive without a reservation, go to one of the VVV tourist offices which can guarantee to find you something, though it may not be in the class or area you prefer. Watch out for hidden pitfalls, such as Golden Age canalhouses with four or five floors, steep, narrow stairways, and no lifts; and tranquil-looking mansions with a late-night café terrace next door.

101

Excursions from the City

Bijou Properties
Wherever possible, the hotels listed in this section have been chosen for having something more in the way of local character than their name. This has often meant selecting hotels in old buildings, some transformed from their original purpose. There are plenty of alternatives, though, if you just want a straightforward modern hotel with few trimmings or an unpretentious budget hotel with even less.

Edam
De Fortuna (€–€€)
Canalside hotel in the heart of town, with a 17th-century main building, garden and up-to-date amenities.
✉ Spuistraat 1–7 ☎ 0299/371 671; fax 0299/371 469; www.fortuna/edam.nl

Delft
De Kok (€–€€)
Four connected mansions form this stylish hotel between the railway station and the old centre. Rooms are modern and there's a large garden with a fountain.
✉ Houttuinen 14 ☎ /fax 015/212 2125; www.hoteldekok.nl

Leeuwenbrug (€€)
In two town-centre canalside buildings, with Old Dutch public rooms and plain but modern guest rooms.
✉ Koornmarkt 16 ☎ 015/214 7741; fax 015/215 9759; www.leeuwenbrug.nl

Den Haag & Scheveningen
Astoria (€)
Small, family-owned hotel near the Hollands Spoor railway station. Facilities are minimal but its rooms are comfortable and clean.
✉ Stationsweg 139, The Hague ☎ 070/384 0401; fax 070/354 1653 🚊 11, 12

Des Indes Inter Continental (€€€)
Height of elegance, in an 1880s baronial mansion. Its rooms are the last word in comfort and amenities, its dining areas fashionable meeting-places.
✉ Lange Voorhout 54–6, The Hague ☎ 070/361 2345; fax 070/345 1721; www.desindes.com 🚊 1, 3, 7, 8, 9, 12

Mercure Den Haag Central (€€)
Big, ultramodern city-centre hotel that makes up in comfort and efficiency what it may lack in character.
✉ Spui 180, The Hague ☎ 070/363 6700; fax 070/363 9398; www.mercure.com 🚊 1, 8, 9, 10, 16, 17

Parkhotel (€€)
Characterful modern hotel with modestly comfortable rooms, on a quiet, embassy-lined street overlooking Zorgvliet Park.
✉ Molenstraat 53, The Hague ☎ 070/362 4371; fax 070/361 4525; www.parkhoteldenhaag.nl 🚊 7

Steigenberger Kurhaus (€€€)
Palatial national monument on the seafront, with luxuriously appointed rooms and smart restaurants and cafés, including the *belle époque* Kurzaal restaurant and concert hall.
✉ Gevers Deynootplein 30, Scheveningen ☎ 070/416 2636; fax 070/416 2646; www.kurhaus.nl 🚊 1, 9

Leiden
Hotel de Doelen (€)
Elegant, small canalside hotel, incorporating a 15th-century merchant's house and retaining some period character.
✉ Rapenburg 2 ☎ 071/512 0527; fax 071/512 8453; www.dedoelen.com 🚊 43

Rotterdam
Bilderberg Parkhotel (€€)
Ultramodern hotel near Centraal Station, with

plushly furnished and well-equipped rooms and a garden restaurant.

✉ **Westersingel 70**
☎ **010/436 3611; fax 010/436 4212; www.bilderberg.nl** 🚊 **5**

New York (€–€€)

An 11-storey 'skyscraper' built between 1897 and 1898 as the Holland-America Line's headquarters is now a hotel that retains some old office fittings and has modern rooms and great harbour views.

✉ **Koninginnenhoofd 1**
☎ **010/439 0500; fax 010/484 2701; www.hotelnewyork.nl**
🚊 **20**

Texel

Koogerend (€€)

Recently renovated, this attractive, red-roofed hotel in the centre of the island's diminutive capital has modern wings built around a traditional house.

✉ **Koogerstraat 94, Den Burg**
☎ **0222/313301; fax 0222/315902; www.fletcher.nl**

Grand Hotel Opduin (€€)

Modern hotel with large, comfortable rooms and a swimming-pool and sauna, behind the sea-defence dunes on the west coast.

✉ **Ruyslaan 22, De Koog**
☎ **0222/317 445; fax 0222/317 777; www.opduin.nl**

Utrecht

Malie (€–€€)

Though out of the centre, this attractive small hotel in two century-old villas has room décor that matches its genteel surroundings.

✉ **Maliestraat 2/4**
☎ **030/231 6424; fax 030/234 0661; www.maliehotel.nl**
🚊 **4, 11**

Park Plaza Utrecht (€€)

Large, modern chain hotel beside the railway station, convenient for the centre. Well-equipped rooms at a good price.

✉ **Westplein 50** ☎ **030/292-5200; fax 030/292-5199; www.parkplazaww.com**
🚉 **Utrecht Station**

Tulip Inn Utrecht

Turn-of-the-19th-century, city-centre hotel with a high standard of facilities and cosy rooms.

✉ **Janskerkhof 10** ☎ **030/231 3169; fax 030/231 0148; www.nh-hotels.com** 🚊 **2, 3, 11, 12, 22**

Volendam

Spaander (€€)

Animated harbourside hotel that mixes old-fashioned country charm with bright, modernly furnished rooms and has a swimming-pool.

✉ **Haven 15–19** ☎ **0299/363 595; fax 0299/369 615; www.bestwestern.nl**

Zandvoort

Golden Tulip Zandvoort (€€)

Zandvoort's finest hotel offers a good package of amenities, including a beachfront location, swimming-pool, sports facilities and modern rooms, at a moderate price.

✉ **Burgomeester van Alphenstraat 63** ☎ **023/571 3234; fax 023/571 9094; www.naarzee.nl**

Zuiderbad (€)

Superior family hotel, with a sea view, plainly furnished but well-equipped rooms and a pavement café.

✉ **Boulevard Paulus Loot 5**
☎ **023/571 2613; fax 023/571 3190; www.hotelzuiderbad.nl**

Bed and Breakfast

If you are touring from Amsterdam and don't want to pre-book a hotel, you'll find lots of B&B accommodation in many areas. Either visit the local VVV tourist office, which will have a comprehensive list of establishments in its area and can book for you, or simply choose a place as you pass by. Some have 'B&B' signs, but they are more usually identified by 'room-free' signs in Dutch: '*Kamer Vrij*'; and German: '*Zimmer Frei*'.

Art, Antiques & Books

Shopping Areas

Many art galleries and antiques shops are concentrated in the Spiegelkwartier along Spiegelgracht and Nieuwe Spiegelstraat. Rokin has more galleries and up-market boutiques, and Kalverstraat, Damrak and Leidsestraat are popular shopping streets. On P C Hooftstraat and Van Baerlestraat you find designer shops. The Jordaan and small connecting streets in the northern canal ring are the places for second-hand shops and off-beat little boutiques. There's a cluster of bookshops on Kalverstraat and around Spui. Warmoesstraat and the Red Light District specialise in erotic goods.

Antiques

Amsterdam Antiques Gallery

A group of six dealers under one roof on the city's main antiques street, selling quality paintings, silver, pewter, Delft blue and more.

✉ **Nieuwe Spiegelstraat 134** ☎ **625 3371** 🚊 6, 7, 10, 20

Kunst–Antiekcentrum De Looier

Rambling art and antiques market in a collection of old warehouses, with 160-plus dealers selling everything from valuable heirlooms to collectable gewgaws.

✉ **Elandsgracht 109** ☎ **624 9038** 🚊 7, 10, 17, 20

Premsela & Hamburger

Dutch royalty gives its seal of approval, and its custom, to this refined setting for antique and contemporary silver and jewellery. Also does repair work.

✉ **Rokin 120** ☎ **624 9688** 🚊 4, 9, 14, 16, 20, 24, 25

Art

De Praktijk

Run by a local enthusiast, this gallery in the Jordaan focuses on moderately priced modern Dutch painting and photography.

✉ **Lauriergracht 96** ☎ **422 1727** 🚊 10, 17, 29

Jaski Art Gallery

Painting, sculpture, graphic works and ceramics by mainly Cobra artists from 1948–51, including works by later artists.

✉ **Nieuwe Spiegelstraat 27–9** ☎ **620 3939** 🚊 6, 7, 10

Books

American Book Center

In addition to its mainstream books, this multi-floor store has strong specialist sections, including gay, erotic, science fiction and fantasy books, as well as second-hand magazines, war-games and sword-and-sorcery games.

✉ **Kalverstraat 185** ☎ **625 5537** 🚊 4, 9, 14, 16, 20, 24, 25

Athenaeum Boekhandel

An art nouveau store from 1904 divided into a warren of nooks and crannies for mainly high-brow books in different languages. The attached Athenaeum Nieuwshandel sells international newspapers and magazines.

✉ **Spui 14–16** ☎ **622 6248** 🚊 1, 2, 5

De Slegte

The city's largest second-hand bookshop has a vast choice of titles in multiple languages on several floors.

✉ **Kalverstraat 48–52** ☎ **622 5933** 🚊 4, 9, 14, 16, 20, 24, 25

Vrolijk Gay and Lesbian Bookstore

Large range of books, primarily in English. Often cheaper than gay sections of mainstream stores.

✉ **Paleisstraat 135** ☎ **623 5142** 🚊 1, 2, 4, 5, 9, 13, 14, 16, 17, 20, 24, 25

Waterstone's

Branch of the British chain, with a huge stock of hardbacks and paperbacks, fiction and non-fiction, for adults and children.

✉ **Kalverstraat 152** ☎ **638 3821** 🚊 1, 2, 5

Gifts & Children's Items

Gifts

BLGK Edelsmeden

Showcase for a group of local jewellery designers, each one with a different contemporary approach, but all making notable pieces at reasonable prices.

✉ Hartenstraat 28 ☎ 624 8154 🚋 13, 14, 17, 20

Blue Gold Fish

Storehouse of fantastical gifts of all sorts, including jewellery, ornaments, home fixtures, fabrics and miscellaneous items that don't fall into any easily defined category.

✉ Rozengracht 17 ☎ 623 3134 🚋 13, 14, 17, 20

Focke & Meltzer

Sells various high-end pottery, glass and other international gift labels, including quality handmade Delft Blue from De Koninklijke Porcelyne Fles and Tichelaars Makkumware porcelain.

✉ Gelderlandplein 149, Buitenveldert ☎ 644 4429 🚋 2, 3, 5, 12, 20

Heinen

Hand-painted De Koninklijke Fles Delft Blue and Tichelaars Makkumware, made by a father-and-son team of craftsmen.

✉ Prinsengracht 440 ☎ 627 8299 🚋 1, 2, 5, 13, 17, 20

Het Kantenhuis

Most lace you can buy in Holland is machine-made, often even in other countries. This shop sells the genuine article – superior, handmade Dutch lace.

✉ Kalverstraat 124 ☎ 624 8618 🚋 4, 9, 14, 16, 20, 24, 25

Parfumerie Douglas

Cut straight to the essence, amid a vast stock of big-name scents alongside other unpretentious concoctions and precocious wannabes.

✉ P C Hooftstraat 107 ☎ 679 5822 🚋 2, 3, 5, 12, 20

La Savonnerie

Get into a lather over designer soap in arty and kitschy forms; it seems a downright shame actually to put some of it in a bath!

✉ Prinsengracht 294 ☎ 428 1139 🚋 13, 14, 17, 20

Children's Wear & Toys

Kinderfeestwinkel

All kinds of fun things for kids to play with and wear at party time.

✉ Eerste van der Helstraat 15 ☎ 470 4791 🚋 16, 24, 25

Mechanisch Speelgoed

Batteries definitely not included in these modern versions of toys from a kinder, gentler era of youthful playthings.

✉ Westerstraat 67 ☎ 638 1680 🚋 3, 10

Oilily

Bright and sporty designer clothes for kids – an instant hit.

✉ P C Hooftstraat 131–3 ☎ 672 3361 🚋 2, 3, 5, 12, 20

Pas-Destoel

Brings interior design skills and a sense of fun to bear on children's furniture, room fittings and accessories.

✉ Westerstraat 260 ☎ 420 7542 🚋 3, 10

Shoppers' Tips

• Most shops are open Mon 1–6 (department stores from 11), Tue–Wed and Fri 9–6, Thu 9–9, Sat 9–5; some are open Sun noon–5.

• For bargains, look out for *solden* (sales) during January and July; stickers on some goods saying *korting* (reduction); and on shop windows *totaal uitverkoop* (clearing out) when a shop is closing down or changing its lines.

• When you walk into a small shop to browse around, remember to greet the owner, a polite gesture Dutch people appreciate.

Department Stores, Malls & Markets

Dutch Gifts
Among items that make great souvenirs and gifts are: tulip bulbs (you may need a phyto-sanitary certificate to import them); bottles of *jenever* (Dutch gin); antiques; diamonds; cheese (not only Edam and Gouda); handmade pralines; crystal from Royal Leerdam; pewter; Delftware and Makkumware porcelain; clogs; prints; and even postcards, from museum shops, depicting paintings and other exhibits.

Department Stores & Malls

De Bijenkorf
Flagship, up-market department store.
✉ **Dam 1** ☎ **621 8080** 🚊 **4, 9, 14, 16, 20, 24, 25**

Hema
Cheap 'n' cheerful bargain basement chain. Good for underwear, household goods and some food items.
✉ **Kalvertoren Shopping Centre, Kalverstraat** ☎ **422 8988** 🚊 **4, 9, 14, 16, 20, 24, 25**

Magna Plaza
The turreted, Gothic, former main post office, known as 'Perenberg' (Pear Mountain), is now a fancy mall with shops and cafés on several floors, including a Virgin Megastore in the basement.
✉ **Spuistraat 168** ☎ **626 9199** 🚊 **1, 2, 5, 13, 14, 17, 20**

Maison de Bonneterie
Up-market store for clothing, shoes, household goods, sports equipment and more.
✉ **Kalverstraat 183/Rokin 140–2** ☎ **626 2162** 🚊 **4, 9, 14, 16, 20, 24, 25**

Metz & Co
This *belle époque* building hosts a quality store with an avant-garde past, though its Rietveld furniture is now reproduction rather than original. Good for fabrics.
✉ **Keizersgracht 455/Leidsestraat 34–6** ☎ **520 7020** 🚊 **1, 2, 5**

Vroom & Dreesman
Clothing, jewellery, perfumes, electronic and household goods.
✉ **Kalverstraat 201–3** ☎ **622 0171** 🚊 **4, 9, 14, 16, 20, 24, 25**

Markets

Albert Cuypmarkt
The city's biggest and most colourful street market: a long double-row of stalls selling foodstuffs, clothes, flowers, cakes and biscuits, household goods and more.
✉ **Albert Cuypstraat** 🕐 **Mon–Sat 9:30–5** 🚊 **4, 16, 24, 25**

Bloemenmarkt
Amsterdam's famous floating Flower Market, on a line of barges beside Muntplein (► 39).
✉ **Singel** 🕐 **Mon–Sat 9:30–5:30 (5 Sat)** 🚊 **4, 9, 14, 16, 20, 24, 25**

Boerenmarkt
Saturday Farmer's Market selling organic produce, bread and cheese, and New Age jewellery, scents and health-care products.
✉ **Noordermarkt** 🕐 **Sat 9–4 (3 in winter)** 🚌 **Bus 18, 22**

Kunstmart Thorbeckepleine
Bijou paintings, pottery and sculpture at an elegant little Sunday art market.
✉ **Thorbeckeplein** 🕐 **Mar–Nov Sun 10:30–6** 🚊 **4, 9, 14, 20**

Waterlooplein Fleemarkt
Once a standby of the city's Jewish community, this big flea market is sure to have something of interest.
✉ **Waterlooplein** 🕐 **Mon–Sat 9–5** 🚇 **Waterlooplein** 🚊 **9, 14, 20**

Westermarkt
Similar to the Albert Cuypmarkt (► above), but on a more intimate scale.
✉ **Westerstraat** 🕐 **Mon–Sat 9–5** 🚊 **3, 10, 18, 22**

Food & Drink

J G Beune
Sells chocolate versions of Amsterdammetjes (the distinctive bollards that stop cars from parking on the pavement) and a colourful array of cakes and other goodies.
✉ Haarlemmerdijk 156–8 ☎ 624 8356 🚋 1, 2, 5, 13, 17, 20

De Bierkoning
You ought to find something to your taste among 950 different kinds of beer from all over the world, many of which come with their own accompanying glass.
✉ Paleisstraat 125 ☎ 625 2336 🚋 1, 2, 5, 13, 14, 17, 20

Eichholtz
Highly regarded delicatessen with Dutch and international specialities.
✉ Leidsestraat 48 ☎ 622 0305 🚋 1, 2, 5

Geels & Co
Heady aromas mark Holland's oldest tea and coffee traders, in a traditional setting with a tea and coffee museum attached.
✉ Warmoesstraat 67 ☎ 624 0683 🚋 4, 9, 14, 16, 20, 24, 25

Hendrikse Patisserie
Purveyors of luscious cakes and pastries to the royal court – and fortunately to ordinary citizens, also.
✉ Overtoom 472 ☎ 618 0472 🚋 1, 6

Jacob Hooij
A medley of fragrant scents greets you as you enter this 1743 apothecary, selling herbs, spices, herbal teas, health foods, natural cosmetics and homeopathic medicines.
✉ Kloveniersburgwal 12 ☎ 624 3041 🚇 Nieuwmarkt

Olivaria
Fine olive oils from around the world
✉ Hazenstraat 2a ☎ 638 3552 🚋 7, 10, 20

Patisserie Pompadour
A vast selection of delectable cakes and pastries, and an elegant tea room in which to consume those that you don't haul away.
✉ Huidenstraat 12 ☎ 623 9554 🚋 1, 2, 5

Vitals Vitamin Advice Shop
Vitamins, minerals and a range of food supplements.
✉ Nieuwe Nieuwstraat 47 ☎ 625 7298 🚋 1, 2, 5, 13, 17, 20

H P De Vreng en Zoon
Decorated with 15,000 miniature bottles, this distillery and liquor store has been producing traditional *jenever* and liqueurs since 1852.
✉ Nieuwendijk 75 ☎ 624 4581 🚋 1, 2, 5, 13, 17, 20

De Waterwinkel
Cool reservoir of the world's bottled waters, from nifty designer H_2O to the aquatic equivalent of finest champagne.
✉ Roelof Hartstraat 10 ☎ 675 5932 🚋 3, 12, 20, 24

Wout Arxhoek
One of the city's best cheese shops, with over 250 different varieties to choose from – imported from around the world as well as Dutch.
✉ Damstraat 19 ☎ 622 9118 🚋 4, 9, 14, 16, 20, 24, 25

Diamonds' Best Friends
Buying diamonds can be a tricky business. Although they are far from being the only reputable diamond shops in Amsterdam, these five provide an 18-carat guarantee of quality:
Amsterdam Diamond Center
✉ Rokin 1–5
☎ 624 5787
🚋 4, 9, 16, 20, 24, 25
Coster Diamonds
✉ Paulus Potterstraat 2–6
☎ 305 5555
🚋 2, 5, 20
Gassan Diamonds
✉ Nieuwe Uilenburgerstraat 173–5
☎ 622 5333
🚇 Waterlooplein
🚋 9, 14, 20
Stoeltie Diamonds
✉ Wagenstraat 13–17
☎ 623 7601
🚇 Waterlooplein
🚋 4, 9, 14, 20
Van Moppes Diamonds
✉ Albert Cuypstraat 2–6
☎ 676 1242
🚋 3, 5, 12, 16, 20, 24, 25

Fashion, Household & Speciality

Tax-free Shopping

If you live outside the European Union, you are entitled to a refund of 13.5 per cent of value-added tax (BTW) on purchases of €137 or more in one shop in a day. You can also make purchases above that amount in other shops, going through the refund process each time. You can identify participating shops by their 'tax-free shopping' stickers. Ask for an Easy Tax Free Cheque when you pay. When you are leaving Holland for a non-EU country, within three months of buying, present the cheque at Customs, who will stamp it. You can claim your refund at the International Cash Refund Office of Global Refund at Schiphol Airport, and by post to Global Refund Holland:

✉ Leidsevaartweg 99, 2106 AS Heemstede, Netherlands ☎ 023/524 1909.

Fashion & Accessories

Candy Corson

All kinds of quality leather accessories, with the emphasis on bags and belts.

✉ Sint-Luciënsteeg 19 ☎ 624 8061 🚋 1, 2, 5

Cora Kemperman

Elegant and imaginative, individually designed women's fashion.

✉ Leidsestraat 72 ☎ 625 1284 🚋 1, 2, 5

Emporio Armani

Exactly as you'd expect, quality and style in Italian clothing.

✉ P C Hooftstraat 39–41 ☎ 471 1121 🚋 2, 3, 5, 12, 20

Hair Police

Hair styling in a variety of street-smart looks, along with more punky fashions, cosmetics and other accessories.

✉ Kerkstraat 113 ☎ 420 5841 🚋 1, 2, 5

Hester van Eeghen

Imaginatively designed leather accessories, including handbags, belts and wallets.

✉ Hartenstraat 1 ☎ 626 9212 🚋 13, 14, 17, 20

The Madhatter

Far-out headwear by local designers.

✉ Van der Helstplein 4 ☎ 664 7748 🚋 3, 12, 25

Oger

Quality men's clothing, including Ermenegildo Zegna.

✉ P C Hooftstraat 79–83 ☎ 676 8695 🚋 2, 3, 5, 12, 20

Palette

Tiny shop with a big choice of well-made shoes in satin and silk.

✉ Nieuwezijds Voorburgwal 125 ☎ 639 3207 🚋 4, 9, 14, 16, 20, 24, 25

Webers Holland

Sexy, humorous and avant-garde fashion, mainly for women.

✉ Kloveniersburgwal 26 ☎ 638 1777 🚋 4, 9, 14, 16, 20, 24, 25

Alternative

Absolute Danny

Erotic clothing and accessories with a sense of style.

✉ Oudezijds Achterburgwal 78 ☎ 421 0915 🚋 4, 9, 14, 16, 20, 24, 25

Condomerie Het Gulden Vlies

The world's first specialist condom shop, the 'Golden Fleece' stocks an impressive range of this singular item of apparel.

✉ Warmoesstraat 141 ☎ 627 4174 🚋 4, 9, 14, 16, 20, 24, 25

The Headshop

Market leader since the heady summer of 1968 in drug paraphernalia and books, oriental clothing, weird and wonderful jewellery, insight into magic mushrooms and more along the same lines.

✉ Kloveniersburgwal 39 ☎ 624 9061 🚇 Nieuwmarkt

Hemp Works

Clothing, cosmetics and more, all made from multipurpose hemp fibre.

✉ Nieuwmarkt 13 ☎ 421 1762 🚋 1, 2, 5, 13, 17, 20

Household

Kitsch Kitchen
If you want your kitchen filled with all kinds of brightly coloured, odd-looking stuff from around the world, this is the place to get it.

✉ **Eerste Bloemdwarsstraat 21** ☎ **428 4969** 🚋 **13, 14, 17, 20**

Outras Coisas
Furnishings and acessories in traditional styles for the home and garden, both new and secondhand, originate from European countries and beyond.

✉ **Herenstraat 31** ☎ **625 7281** 🚋 **1, 2, 5, 13, 17, 20**

Wonen 2000
You likely won't be able to haul away many of the larger items from this vast depository of designer furniture, but the range of portable accessories is extensive too.

✉ **Rozengracht 219–223** ☎ **521 8710** 🚋 **13, 14, 17, 20**

World of Wonders
Interior design store in the fast-gentrifying Eastern Docks, with up-market fabrics and furnishings, and many small items to enliven your living space.

✉ **KNSM-laan 293–9** ☎ **418 4067** 🚌 **Bus 32**

Speciality

Animation Art
Drawings, paintings and figurines of famous cartoon characters from Superman to Tintin and the Smurfs.

✉ **Berenstraat 19** ☎ **627 7600** 🚋 **1, 2, 5**

Bankras
One of the best bicycle shops in this bike-mad city.

✉ **Nieuwe Hoogstraat 21–3** ☎ **624 6137** 🚇 **Nieuwmarkt**

Capsicum
Fabrics to go – anywhere and with anything. Choose from delicate material for summer dresses to hard-wearing furniture covers.

✉ **Oude Hoogstraat 1** ☎ **623 1016** 🚋 **4, 9, 14, 16, 20, 24, 25**

Cortina Paper
The paper chase ends here, in a stockpile of all kinds of fine paper, including handmade, as well as notebooks and other writing and sketching materials.

✉ **Reestraat 22** ☎ **623 6676** 🚋 **13, 14, 17, 20**

P G C Hajenius
Treats smoking reverently rather than as a social nuisance, with a big range of pipes and cigar humidors.

✉ **Rokin 92–6** ☎ **623 7494** 🚋 **4, 9, 14, 16, 20, 24, 25**

Hera Kaarsen
Candles that it seems a pity to burn, many of them being works of waxen art designed by the owners.

✉ **Overtoom 402** ☎ **616 2886** 🚋 **1, 6**

De Knopen Winkel
The Button Shop has 8,000 different kinds of these handy items in stock.

✉ **Wolvenstraat 14** ☎ **624 0479** 🚋 **1, 2, 5**

Otten & Zn
Some Dutch people still clomp around in wooden *klompen* (clogs). This shop sells fine wearable ones as well as souvenirs.

✉ **Eerste van der Helststraat 31** ☎ **662 9724** 🚋 **16, 24, 25**

Fast Getaways
If you don't want to spend your valuable time in the city shopping, and if you're leaving from Schiphol Airport, do it there. With 40 shops stocking 120,000 different items in the airport's duty-free section, and another 40 non-duty-free shops at Schiphol Plaza, there's no shortage of choice.

Attractions for Children

Getting Around

Trams are a must, in particular older trams in which kids can stand beside the driver. Canal boat cruises and free passenger ferries behind Centraal Station can also be fun.

Should you let children cycle? There are bicycle lanes, but there are also trams, heavy traffic, lots of other cyclists, and unthinking pedestrians. It may be safer to take them on an out-of-town cycling trip, such as the one to Ouderkerk aan de Amstel (► 85).

Museums

The Rijksmuseum's Golden Age masterpieces (► 22–3) may glaze youthful eyes after the first couple of hundred. Child-friendly exhibits, such as model sailing ships and beautifully made doll's houses, should go down better.

Older children will appreciate the special atmosphere at the Anne Frankhuis, the teenage Jewish diarist's wartime hideaway (► 17). Younger ones are liable to be bored, as there is not much to see.

Sail in youthful imagination to the fabled Spice Islands aboard a replica 17th-century Dutch East Indiaman at the Nederlands Scheepvaartmuseum (► 60), and in summer watch actors re-create scenes of onboard life. Interactive science and technology museum NEMO (► 61), and Kindermuseum (☎ 568 8300), the children-only section of the Tropenmuseum (► 73), should fascinate switched-on children.

If your flight from Schiphol airport is delayed, you could take the kids to the Aviodome aviation museum at the airport (► 38).

Children's Farms and Zoos

Artis (► 35), as well as being a great zoo, has a children's farm with goats, a cow, a donkey and chickens, where children get an insight into life on a real farm. The same experience applies to a children's farm in the Pijp district, Kinderboerderij De Pijp (✉ Lizzy Ansinghstraat 82 ☎ 664 8303 🕐 Mon–Fri 11–5, Sat–Sun 1–5 🚊 12, 25).

Places of Interest

In addition to such Dutch favourites as soccer hotshot Johann Cruyff, there's a gallery of waxwork international names at Madame Tussaud's (► 56). Many city-centre bell towers have carillons that break into tinkling song at intervals. You can hear carillon concerts at the Westertoren (► 26 – 🕐 Tue noon–1); Zuidertoren (► 75 – 🕐 Thu noon–1); Munttoren (► 57 – 🕐 Fri noon–1); Oude Kerkstoren (► 63 – 🕐 Sat 4–5). Open-Air Chess (✉ Max Euweplein), off Leidseplein, played with big plastic pieces, should appeal to cerebral exhibitionists. For shoot-'em-up action, try Intersphere Lasergames (✉ Prins Hendrikkade 194 ☎ 622 4809 🚊 22, 32). White-knuckle go-kart racing thrills are on offer at Kartbaan Amsterdam (✉ Theemsweg 19, Sloterdijk ☎ 611 1642 🚊 12).

Beach and Sea

Zandvoort (➤ 89) is Amsterdam's closest and busiest resort and has a great beach, safe bathing and lots to do. Resorts north of Zandvoort are quieter, with fewer amenities.

The freshwater IJsselmeer lake (➤ 84) used to be a sea. It's not ideal for swimming, although paddling in shallow water should be alright, but there are old harbours, traditional sailing ships, boat excursions, and waterside things to see and do.

Windmills

Amsterdam is not well-endowed with these emblematic sights. You'd do better at nearby De Zaanse Schans (➤ 88), and even better to make the longer trip to Kinderdijk (➤ 87), near Rotterdam.

Flowers

Taking the kids to the Bulb Fields (➤ 78), Keukenhof Garden (➤ 78), and the Floating Flower Market (➤ 106) will probably turn out to be one of those gender things. Boys will probably love them and girls hate them – you never know, it could happen.

Sports

For swimming, ice-skating, fishing, and more (➤ 115).

Theme Parks

Archeon

Step into the past at this archaeological theme park between Amsterdam and Rotterdam, which re-creates scenes from Stone Age, ancient Roman and medieval life, and tells the story of the Earth from its formation.

✉ Archeonlaan 1, Alphen aan den Rijn ☎ 0172/447 744 🕐 May–Oct Tue–Sun 10–5; Jul–Aug daily 10–6 🚉 Alphen aan de Rijn ♿ Good 💶 Very expensive

Dolfinarium Harderwijk

Europe's largest dolphinarium puts on fabulous shows, runs research programmes and has a rehabilitation centre for sick and injured creatures. In addition to open-air pools there are glass tanks where you can view the performers underwater.

✉ Strandboulevard Oost 1, Harderwijk ☎ 0341/467 400 🕐 Mid-Feb–Oct daily 10–6 🚉 Harderwijk ♿ Good 💶 Very expensive

De Efteling

Rather further afield, near Den Bosch in southern Holland, De Efteling is one of Europe's oldest theme parks with rides and roller-coasters and the fairytale forest for younger children.

✉ Europalaan 2, Kaatsheuvel ☎ 0416/288 111 🕐 Apr–Oct, daily 10–6 (mid–Jul to end Aug till midnight) 💶 Expensive

Circus

If you don't think your children can perform enough tricks already, let them learn tightrope walking, juggling and other circus tricks at Circus Elleboog.

✉ Passeerdersgracht 32 ☎ 626 9370 🕐 Mon–Fri 10–5, Sat 1:30–5, Sun 10:30–4 🚋 7, 10, 20 There are mime and puppet shows at nearby De Krakeling Theater.

✉ Nieuwe Passeerdersstraat 1 ☎ 625 3824 🕐 Mon–Fri 11–4, Sat–Sun 2–7 🚋 7, 10, 20

Eating Out

There are McDonalds, Burger King, KFC and Pizza Hut outlets all over town. For a different kind of taste sensation, where children aged five to 12 cook for themselves supervised by adults, take them to Kinderkookkafé (✉ Oudezijds Achterburgwal 193 ☎ 625 3257 🕐 Sat cooking 3:30–6, dinner 6–8 (age 8 plus); Sun cooking 2:30–5, high tea 5–6 (age 5 plus); Mon–Fri 1–3 🚉 Nieuwmarkt 🚋 4, 9, 14, 16, 20, 24, 25).

Music, Theatre, Dance & Cinema

Information and Tickets

For information on, and tickets for, events at most city venues, visit Amsterdams Uit Buro (AUB) ✉ Leidseplein 26 🕐 Daily 10–6 (Thu until 9) 🚊 1, 2, 5, 6, 7, 10, 20; or call the AUB-Uitlijn ☎ 0900/0191 🕐 Daily 9–9. You can also buy tickets at VVV tourist offices.

For programme information, the VVV's monthly English-language guide, *What's On in Amsterdam*, provides extensive listings across the range of cultural events, as does the free monthly Dutch *Uitkrant*, which you find at many venues.

Beurs van Berlage

Home of the Netherlands Philharmonic Orchestra and Netherlands Chamber Orchestra, in the former stock exchange.
✉ Damrak 243 ☎ 521 7500 🕐 Box office: Tue–Fri 12:30–6, Sat 12:30–5, and 1¼ hours before performances 🚊 4, 9, 14, 16, 20, 24, 25

Concertgebouw

Home of the famed Royal Concertgebouw Orchestra. Its Grote Zaal is considered one of the world's most acoustically perfect concert halls; the Kleine Zaal is used mainly for chamber music and recitals. Free concerts on Wednesdays at 12:30.
✉ Concertgebouwplein 2–6 ☎ 671 8345 🕐 Box office: daily 10–5 for advance purchase 🚊 3, 5, 12, 16, 20

De IJsbreker

The place for contemporary, electronic, experimental, cutting-edge music.
✉ Weesperzijde 23 ☎ 693 9093 🕐 Box office: Mon–Fri 10–5 🚊 Weesperplein 🚊 3, 6, 7, 10, 20

Muziektheater

Home of the Netherlands Opera and National Ballet, and Amsterdam venue for performances by The Hague's highly regarded Netherlands Dance Theatre.
✉ Amstel 1–3 ☎ 625 5455 🕐 Box office: Mon–Sat 10–6, Sun 11:30–6 🚊 Waterlooplein 🚊 9, 14, 20

Recitals

Engelse Kerk
✉ Begijnhof 48 ☎ 624 9665 🚊 1, 2, 5

Nieuwe Kerk
✉ Dam ☎ 638 6909 🚊 1, 2, 4, 5, 9, 13, 14, 16, 17, 20, 24, 25

Oude Kerk
✉ Oudekerksplein 23 ☎ 625 8284 🚊 4, 9, 14, 16, 20, 24, 25

Sweelinck Conservatorium
✉ Van Baerlestraat 27 ☎ 527 7550 🚊 3, 5, 12, 20

Waalse Kerk
✉ Oudezijds Achterburgwal 157 ☎ 623 2074 🚊 4, 9, 14, 16, 20, 24, 25

Theatre, Dance & Musicals

Boom Chicago Theater
Improvisational comedy in English, over drinks/dinner.
✉ Leidseplein 12 ☎ 423 0101 🕐 Summer: daily from 7; winter: Mon–Sat from 7 🚊 1, 2, 5, 6, 7, 10, 20

Koninklijke Theater Carré
Dutch versions of big-name musicals, cabaret, pop music.
✉ Amstel 115–25 ☎ 0800/2525 255 🕐 Box office: Mon–Sat 10–7, Sun 1–7 🚊 Weesperplein 🚊 4, 6, 7, 10, 20

Stadsschouwburg
Mainstream Dutch theatre, and an occasional touring performance in English. Also hosts opera and dance.
✉ Leidseplein 26 ☎ 624 2311 🕐 Mon–Sat 10AM–6; Sun & pub hols from 90 mins before performance 🚊 1, 2, 5, 6, 7, 10, 20

Vondelpark Openluchttheater
Open-air theatre, music and dance in summer.
✉ Vondelpark ☎ 523 7700 🚊 1, 2, 3, 5, 6, 12, 20 💷 Free

Live Music

Alto Jazz Café
Wide-ranging music from resident and visiting combos.
✉ **Korte Leidsedwarsstraat 115** ☎ 626 3249 🚋 1, 2, 5, 6, 7, 10, 20

Bimhuis
The place for serious lovers of improvisational jazz.
✉ **Oudeschans 73–7** ☎ 623 1361 🚇 **Waterlooplein** 🚋 9, 14, 20

De Heeren van Aemstel
Upper-crust café where you occasionally catch some big names at their session on Wednesday at 9:30.
✉ **Thorbeckeplein 5** ☎ 620 2173 🚋 4, 9, 14, 20

Maloe Melo
Cosy, smoky den that serves up some fine blues.
✉ **Lijnbaansgracht 163** ☎ 420 4592 🚋 7, 10, 17, 20

Dance Clubs & Discos

Akhnaton
World music, salsa, rap and reggae.
✉ **Nieuwezijds Kolk 25** ☎ 624 3396 🚋 1, 2, 5, 13, 17, 20

Club Arena
In the atmospheric and extensive setting of a former orphanage chapel (▶ 100), dance to a mix of funk, soul and galactic disco. Friday and Saturday are the nostalgia evenings, with music dating from as far back as the '60s.
✉ **'s Gravesandestraat 51** ☎ 633 3021 🚋 3, 7, 10

iT
Mainly, though not exclusively, gay dance club, with techno and house in a wild-party atmosphere.
✉ **Amstelstraat 24** ☎ 625 0111 🚋 4, 9, 14, 20

Odeon
Dance club in a 17th-century canalhouse; different disco styles on different floors.
✉ **Singel 460** ☎ 624 9711 🚋 1, 2, 5

Paradiso
Rock, reggae and pop, live and disco, in a former church.
✉ **Weteringschans 6–8** ☎ 626 4521 🚋 1, 2, 5, 6, 7, 10, 20

The Back Door
Late-night house.
✉ **Amstelstraat 28–32** ☎ 620 2333 🚋 4, 9, 14, 20

Rock Music
Big names perform at Ajax soccer club's Amsterdam ArenA stadium (▶ 115); less-big acts at Koninklijke Theater Carré (▶ 112).

Cinemas
Most films are shown in their original language with Dutch subtitles.

City
Seven screens just off Leidseplein.
✉ **Kleine Gartmanplantsoen 13–25** ☎ 623 4579 🚋 1, 2, 5, 6, 7, 10, 20

Nederlands Filmmuseum Cinematheek
International, art-house and rarely screened films.
✉ **Vondelpark 3** ☎ 589 1400 🚋 1, 2, 3, 5, 6, 12, 20

Tuschinski Theater
Superb, art deco cinema complex with six screens.
✉ **Reguliersbreestraat 26–8** ☎ 626 2633 🚋 4, 9, 14, 20

The Milky Way
It's not easy to define De Melkweg, a multipurpose, multimedia, multicultural club in an old dairy factory – hence the name. It started life as a hippie hangout during the 1960s and has kept up with most cultural trends in the city ever since. Alphabetically speaking, it's an art centre, café, dance hall, discothèque, exhibition space, library, restaurant and theatre.
Philosophically speaking, it's a temple of alternative culture. You need to take out a cheap, temporary membership to get in.
✉ **Lijnbaansgracht 234a** ☎ 531 8181 🚋 1, 2, 5, 6, 7, 10, 20

Brown Cafés & Proeflokalen

Gay Amsterdam
The city takes some pride in its status as Europe's gay capital, and there are many clubs, cafés and resources for gay and lesbian residents and visitors. For information, contact the gay people's organisation COC (✉ Rozenstraat 14 ☎ 623 4079 🚊 13, 14, 17, 20, or the Gay and Lesbian Switchboard ☎ 623 6565).

Brown Cafés
A *bruine kroeg* (brown café) is an old-style Amsterdam bar, with walls smoked brown over the centuries, an unhurried approach to life, and almost a guarantee of friendly conversation.

De Druif
Nautically oriented waterfront bar from 1631 in the Eastern Dock area.
✉ **Rapenburgerplein 83**
☎ **624 4530** 🚌 **Bus 22**

De Engelbewaarder
Jazz on Sunday from 4PM livens up a usually tranquil, arty hang-out.
✉ **Kloveniersburgwal 59**
☎ **625 3772** 🚇 **Nieuwmarkt**
🚊 **4, 9, 14, 16, 20, 24, 25**

Hoppe
Standing room only when young professionals and barfly academics drop in for a quick one, or two, after work. Dates from 1670.
✉ **Spuistraat 18–20** ☎ **420 4420** 🚊 **1, 2, 5**

De Karpershoek
Doesn't seem to have changed much since opening in 1629, when its customers were herring packers, sailors and dockers.
✉ **Martelaarsgracht 2** ☎ **624 7886** 🚊 **1, 2, 5, 13, 17, 20**

't Loosje
Turn-of-the-19th-century bar that used to be a horse-drawn tram waiting room.
✉ **Nieuwmarkt 32–4** ☎ **627 2635** 🚇 **Nieuwmarkt**

Papeneiland
Traditional Amsterdam café, seemingly unchanged since 1642.
✉ **Prinsengracht 2** ☎ **624**

1989 🚌 **Bus 18, 22**

De Reiger
Artists, students and others of that ilk are the main customers of this restful Jordaan watering-hole.
✉ **Nieuwe Leliestraat 34**
☎ **624 7426** 🚊 **10, 13, 14, 17, 20**

Reijnders
Traditional café on Leidse-plein, a square where antique charm has mostly given way to modern frenzy.
✉ **Leidseplein 6** ☎ **623 4419**
🚊 **1, 2, 5, 6, 7, 10, 20**

't Smalle
Originally a *proeflokaal* (► below), this cosy café has a terrace on the canal.
✉ **Egelantiersgracht 12**
☎ **623 9617** 🚊 **13, 14, 17**

Tabac
Tiny, wood-floored café on the corner of Prinsengracht.
✉ **Brouwersgracht 101**
☎ **622 4413** 🚌 **Bus 18, 22**

Proeflokalen
'Tasting houses' were established by *jenever* distillers to allow customers a free sample before buying. Today, sadly, you have to pay.

De Drie Fleschjes
Rows of padlocked wooden kegs line a wall in the 'Three Little Bottles', from 1650.
✉ **Gravenstraat 18** ☎ **624 8443** 🚊 **1, 2, 4, 5, 9, 13, 14, 16, 20, 24, 25**

De Ooievaar
Holland's smallest tasting house produces and sells its own-brand *jenevers*.
✉ **Sint Olofspoort 1** ☎ **420 8004** 🚊 **1, 2, 4, 5, 9, 13, 16, 17, 20, 24, 25**

Sport

Cricket

Amsterdamse Cricket Club & VRA
Watch the city's two cricket teams in action on alternate summer Sundays.
✉ **Nieuwe Kalfjeslaan 21b, Amsterdamse Bos** ☎ 643 4438 🚌 Bus 170, 171, 172

Fitness
These two fitness centres have gym, sauna, solarium and aerobics classes.

Fitness Aerobic Center Jansen
✉ **Rokin 109–11** ☎ 626 9366 🕐 Mon–Fri 10AM–10:30PM, Sat–Sun 12–8 🚊 4, 9, 14, 16, 20, 24, 25

A Bigger Splash
✉ **Looiersgracht 26–30** ☎ 624 8484 🕐 7AM to midnight 🚊 7, 10, 20

Football

Ajax
Amsterdam's crack soccer squad play at a superb new stadium in Amsterdam Zuidoost.
✉ **Amsterdam ArenA, ArenA Boulevard** ☎ 311 1333 🚇 Bijlmer

Golf

Golfbaan Waterland
An 18-hole course in Amsterdam Noord.
✉ **Buikslotermeerdijk 141** ☎ 636 1010 🚌 Bus 30

Horse-riding

Amsterdamse Manege
Out-of-town riding school.
✉ **Nieuwe Kalfjeslaan 25, Amsterdamse Bos** ☎ 643 1342 🚌 Bus 170, 171, 172

Hollandsche Manege
Opened in 1882 and inspired by Vienna's Spanish Riding School.
✉ **Vondelstraat 140** ☎ 618 0942 🚊 1, 6

Ice-skating
Canals often freeze in winter, turning waterways into a skating rink.

Jaap Eden Baan
Big outdoor circuit, with a side area for beginners.
✉ **Radioweg 64** ☎ 694 9894 🚊 9

Swimming

Marnixbad
Regular-shaped, public pool.
✉ **Marnixplein 9** ☎ 625 4843 🚊 3, 10

De Mirandabad
Clear-roofed building with wave machines, slides and other amenities.
✉ **De Mirandalaan 9** ☎ 642 8080 🚊 25

Tennis

Amstelpark Tenniscentrum
Holland's biggest, with 42 outdoor and 10 indoor courts; all outdoor ones are floodlit for night play.
✉ **Koenenkade 8, Amsterdamse Bos** ☎ 301 0700 🚌 Bus 170, 171, 172

Squash

Squash City
Plenty of courts near Centraal Station.
✉ **Ketelmakersstraat 6** ☎ 626 7883 🚉 Centraal Station 🚌 Bus 18, 22

Big Freeze
In years when the canals freeze, you may not have to 'restrict' yourself to skating through the city on these sparkling highways. Many Amsterdammers tour through the countryside and even skate on the IJsselmeer when the ice is solid enough. If you are tempted to join them, a good rule is never to go where Dutch people fear to skate – they have a lot of experience and know, usually, when conditions are safe.

What's On When

Amsterdam Arts Adventure

Amsterdam's main cultural season runs from September until June, which used to mean that the city was a cultural desert at the busiest time of the year for tourism. Arts Adventure fills the gap with a varied programme of mostly informal, often open-air, music, theatre and dance events from June to August. For information, contact VVV tourist offices and Amsterdam Uit Buro (► 112).

North Sea Jazz Festival

If you need an excuse to visit The Hague, this annual three-day shindig at the city's Congresgebouw during July could be it. You'll hear many – if not most – of the big international names in jazz and blues, with more than a hundred concerts. For more information, contact the organisers: ☎ 015/215 7756; www.northseajazz.nl.

February

Pre-Lenten Carnival (early February): Amsterdam's has had a less than chequered career, because carnival-goers prefer Maastricht's.

March

Stille Omgang (Sunday nearest March 15): Catholic procession celebrating the 1345 'Miracle of the Host'. Keukenhof Garden (late March–late May): Beautiful gardens at Lisse open (► 78), as tulips and other spring flowers blossom.

April

National Museum Weekend (mid-month): Museums offer free or reduced-price admission.
World Press Photo Awards (Monday, mid-April): Amsterdam-based annual photojournalism prizes and exhibitions.
Haarlem Bloemencorso (last Saturday): Tulip season cortège from Noordwijk to Haarlem.
Koninginnedag (April 30): Queen Beatrix's official birthday – massive street parties and free markets.

May

Herdenkingsdag (May 4): Remembrance Day for World War II victims; two-minute silence at 8PM.
Bevrijdingsdag (May 5): Liberation Day celebrations; a less frenetic version of Koninginnedag.
National Windmill Day (second Saturday): Windmills open to the public and spin their sails.
Vlaggetjesdag (last Saturday): Flag Day fishing-boat race at Scheveningen (► 81) to bring back the season's first new herring for the Queen.

June

Open Garden Days (mid-June): Private canalhouse gardens on Herengracht, Keizersgracht and Prinsengracht open to the public.
Holland Festival (throughout June): International arts festival in Amsterdam, The Hague, Rotterdam and Utrecht.

July

Amsterdam Arts Adventure: ► panel.
North Sea Jazz Festival: ► panel.

August

Prinsengracht Concert (penultimate Saturday): Pulitzer Hotel hosts classical music concert on a canal barge.
Uitmarkt (last weekend): Cultural venues preview the new season.

September

Bloemencorso (first Saturday): Flower parade from Aalsmeer to Amsterdam.
Open Monumentendag (second Saturday): Monuments and buildings that are usually closed or only partly open, are open.

November

Sinterklaas (third Saturday): Holland's Santa Claus parades through town.

December

Pakjesavond (December 5): Holland's traditional day for giving presents.
Oudejaarsavond (December 31): Partying in the street and fireworks.

Practical Matters

Above: *bikes to go at a rental shop*
Right: *Canal Bus route map*

| GMT 12 noon | Amsterdam 1PM | Germany 1PM | USA (NY) 7AM | Spain 1PM |

BEFORE YOU GO

WHAT YOU NEED

		UK	Germany	USA	Spain
● Required ○ Suggested ▲ Not required	Some countries require a passport to remain valid for a minimum period (usually at least six months) beyond the date of entry – contact their consulate or embassy or your travel agent for details.				
Passport/National Identity Card		●	●	●	●
Visa		▲	▲	▲	▲
Onward or Return Ticket		▲	▲	▲	▲
Health Inoculations		▲	▲	▲	▲
Health Documentation (reciprocal agreement document, ▶ 123, Health)		●	●	●	●
Travel Insurance		○	○	○	○
Driving Licence (national)		●	●	●	●
Car Insurance Certificate (if own car)		○	○	○	○
Car Registration Document (if own car)		●	●	●	●

WHEN TO GO

Amsterdam

■ High season
☐ Low season

5°C	6°C	9°C	12°C	16°C	19°C	21°C	22°C	18°C	13°C	9°C	6°C
JAN	FEB	MAR	APR	MAY	JUN	JUL	AUG	SEP	OCT	NOV	DEC

 Wet   Cloud   Snow   Sun   Sunshine/Showers

TOURIST OFFICES

In the UK
Netherlands Board of
Tourism (NBT)
PO Box 30783
London WC2B 6DH
☎ 0207 539 7953
fax: 0207 539 7953
www.holland.com/uk

In the USA
Netherlands Board of
Tourism (NBT)
355 Lexington Avenue
New York
NY 10017
☎ 212/370 7360
fax: 212/370 9507
www.holland.com/us

c/o Northwest Airlines
11101 Aviation Boulevard
Los Angeles
CA 90045
☎ 310/348 9339
fax: 310/348 9344
www.holland.com/us

POLICE 112

FIRE 112

ANY EMERGENCY (including AMBULANCE) 112

ROAD ASSISTANCE (ANWB Wegenwacht) 0800 0888

WHEN YOU ARE THERE

ARRIVING

There are direct flights from Europe and North America. Dutch airline KLM (☎ 474 7747) has scheduled flights from Britain, mainland Europe, North America and beyond, to Amsterdam Airport Schiphol. There are ferry services between Britain and IJmuiden, Rotterdam Europoort and Hoek van Holland. High-speed trains connect Amsterdam with Paris, Brussels and Cologne, and there are international trains and buses from many European cities.

Amsterdam Airport Schiphol	Journey times
Distance to city centre	
12 kilometres	14–19 minutes
	20 minutes
	30 minutes

MONEY

Euro banknotes and coins were introduced in January 2002. There are banknotes for 5, 10, 20, 50, 100, 200 and 500 euros, and coins for 1, 2, 5, 10, 20 and 50 cents, and 1 and 2 euros.

Change money at banks and bureaux de change. Grenswisselkantoor (GWK), with exchange offices at Schiphol airort, Centraal Station and many other main railway stations, ports and motorway border crossings offer fair deals but other bureaux de change may not. Although traveller's cheques are accepted at some hotels, restaurants and shops, it is more advantageous to change them at banks or GWK offices. Eurocheques are no longer accepted.

TIME

 Holland is on Central European Time (GMT+1). Dutch Summer Time (GMT+2) operates from late March, when clocks are put forward one hour, until late October.

CUSTOMS

 CUSTOMS ALLOWANCES

Goods Bought Outside the EU (Duty-Free Limits):
Alcohol: 1 litre of spirits over 22% volume, OR 2 litres of fortified wine, sparkling wine or other liqueurs, PLUS 2 litres of still table wine
Tobacco: 200 cigarettes, OR 100 cigarillos, OR 50 cigars, OR 250g of tobacco
Perfume: 50ml
Toilet water: 250ml

Goods Bought Inside the EU for Your Own Use (Guidance Levels):
Alcohol: 10 litres of spirits, AND 20 litres of fortified wine, sparkling wine or other liqueurs, AND 90 litres of wine, AND 110 litres of beer
Tobacco: 800 cigarettes, AND 400 cigarillos, AND 200 cigars, AND 1kg of tobacco

(For tobacco and alcohol allowances visitors must be 17 and over)

 NO
Drugs, firearms, ammunition, offensive weapons, obscene material, unlicensed animals.

TOURIST OFFICES

Holland Tourist Information (HTi)
Schiphol Plaza
Amsterdam Airport Schiphol
☎ 0900/400 4040
🕐 Daily 7AM–10PM

VVV (Vereiniging voor Vreemdelingen Verkeer) is the universal name for Holland's tourist information organisations, with offices in every city and town.

VVV Amsterdam
✉ Postbus 3901
1001 AS Amsterdam
☎ 0900/400 4040
Fax: 625 2869
www.visitamsterdam.nl

Centraal Station
Platform 1 & Stationsplein 10
🕐 Daily 9–5 (later during summer and other peak periods)

Leidseplein 1
🕐 Daily 9–5 (later during summer and other peak periods)

Stadionplein
🕐 Mon–Sat 9–5 (later during summer and other peak periods)

NATIONAL HOLIDAYS

J	F	M	A	M	J	J	A	S	O	N	D
1		(3)	1(4)	1(3)	2						2

1 Jan	New Year's Day
Mar/Apr	Good Friday, Easter Sunday, Easter Monday
Apr/May	Ascension Day
30 Apr	Queen's Day
5 May	Liberation Day
May/Jun	Whit Sunday, Whit Monday
25 Dec	Christmas Day
26 Dec	Second Day of Christmas

Banks, businesses, most shops and some museums close on these days.

OPENING HOURS

○ Shops	● Museums/monuments
● Offices	○ Churches
● Banks	● Pharmacies

| 9 AM | 10 AM | 11 AM | 12 PM | 1 PM | 2 PM | 3 PM | 4 PM | 5 PM | 6 PM |

In addition to the times shown above, some shops close between noon and 2PM and all day Sunday and Monday, some do not open until 2PM on Monday, many stay open until 9PM on Thursday and close at 5PM on Saturday. Department stores and many other city-centre shops open from noon until 5PM on Sunday. Most supermarkets are open Monday to Friday from 8AM until 8PM, and 6PM on Saturday. Some food shops, often selling delicatessen food and cooked meals to take away in addition to foodstuffs, open from 5PM until midnight. Some banks close at 4PM rather than 5PM, some stay open until 7PM on Thursday, and some open on Saturday. Government offices open Monday to Friday from 8:30PM until 4PM.

DRIVE ON THE RIGHT

TOILETS CHARGE

★★
★★

PUBLIC TRANSPORT

 Internal Flights Distances between Dutch cities are so short that air travel is rarely worth while, but KLM subsidiaries KLM Cityhopper and KLM Exel connect Amsterdam, Eindhoven, Enschede, Groningen and Maastricht.

 Trains Trains are the best way to get to many nearby destinations and for travel throughout the country. Nederlandse Spoorwegen trains are clean and punctual and its Intercity (IC) trains are fast.

 Trams It's hard to imagine Amsterdam without trams. The city's transport company, the Gemeentevoorvoerbedrijf (GVB), runs 17 tram lines; these include Circle Tram 20, which connects most major attractions. For public transport information, call (+ 0900 9292).

Buses GVB buses complement the tram network and cover many points that trams don't serve. NZH buses handle regional services; they are generally slower than trains to common destinations, but serve many places that trains don't.

 Metro There are four Metro lines: 50, 51, 53 and 54. These lines serve the suburbs and are generally not useful for points within the city centre, except for Nieuwmarkt, which has no tram or bus service, and Waterlooplein.

 Boat Most canal boats are touring rather than transport options. For that you need Canal Bus (☎ 623 9886), Museum Boat (☎ 530 1090), which connects many popular museums and other attractions, and Water Taxi (☎ 530 1090).

CAR RENTAL

 The leading international companies have offices at Schiphol Airport and in town. Driving in Amsterdam is not recommended, as the city's narrow streets are congested, parking charges are high to discourage cars, and the penalties are high.

TAXIS

 Generally you cannot hail taxis on the street, although some will stop if you do. You can pick up taxis at the airport, main railway stations, busy city locations and outside bigger hotels. To call a cab, ring Taxi Centrale (☎ 677 7777).

DRIVING

 Speed limits on motorways (snelwegen) are 100km/h on ring roads, approaches to towns, and other busy stretches; 120km/h on other sections.

 Speed limits on country roads are 80km/h.

 Speed limits on urban roads are 50km/h.

 Seatbelts must be worn in front seats at all times and in rear seats where fitted.

 Random breath-testing frequent. Limit 0.05 per cent alcohol in blood.

 Petrol (benzine), which is more expensive than in neighbouring countries, is sold as Super: 98-octane leaded (lood); Super plus: 98-octane unleaded (loodvrij); and Euro: 95-octane unleaded. Diesel and liquid petroleum gas (autogas) are also available.

 If your car breaks down, contact ANWB Wegenwacht (+ 0800/0888). On motorways use the yellow-coloured emergency phones (every 2km) to contact the emergency breakdown service.

PERSONAL SAFETY

Opportunistic theft, such as pickpocketing and stealing from distracted or careless people, is prevalent and tourists are a prime target. Robbery with violence is much rarer, but still take sensible precautions:

- Avoid quiet places at night, particularly if you are alone.
- Watch out for your removables on trams, at Centraal Station, Schiphol Airport, in popular museums, at markets, and on the beach.
- Leave nothing visible in your car to tempt a thief.

Police (*politie*) assistance:
☎ **112**
from any call box

ELECTRICITY

The power supply in Amsterdam is 220 volts Sockets accept two-round-pin plugs. An adaptor is needed for most non-Continental appliances and a voltage transformer for appliances operating on 100–120 volts; exceptions are shavers that use 110-volt sockets you find in many hotel rooms.

TELEPHONES

Most public telephones accept KPN Telecom phonecards (*telefoonkaarten*) of €5, €12.50 and €25; some accept coins of 5, 10, 20 and 30 cents and €1 and €2; some accept both phonecards and

coins; and some accept credit cards. You can buy phonecards at KPN teleboutiques, post offices, station ticket counters and many newsagents. To call the international operator dial 0800 0410.

International Dialling Codes

From Amsterdam to:

UK:	**00 44**
Germany:	**00 49**
USA:	**00 1**
Spain:	**00 34**

POST

Post offices
Most PTT post offices (*postkaantoren*) are open Mon–Fri 9–5. Hoofdpostkantoor (head post office):
✉ Singel 250–256
☎ 330 0555 🕐
Mon–Wed & Fri 9–6, Thu 9–8, Sat 9–1.

TIPS/GRATUITIES

Yes ✓ No ✗		
Hotels (service included)	✓	change
Restaurants (service included)	✓	change
Cafés (service included)	✓	change
Taxis (service included)	✓	10%
Tour guides	✓	€1/€5
Porters (charge)	✓	change
Chambermaids	✓	€3/€5
Usherettes	✗	
Hairdressers	✓	change
Cloakroom attendants	✗	
Toilets (charge)	✗	

PHOTOGRAPHY

Light: although Amsterdam can be hazy, North Sea breezes usually sweep this haze away. After a summer shower the air has a sparkling, luminous quality. Where you can photograph: some museums and other attractions do not allow you to take photographs; some forbid you to use flash; for some you need permission before you can use a tripod-mounted camera. Where to buy film: film and camera batteries are readily available from photographic and tourist shops. Slides are called dias.

HEALTH

 Insurance Nationals of EU countries can obtain free medical treatment in the Netherlands with the relevant documentation (Form E111 for British citizens), although 10 per cent of prescribed medicine must be paid for. Private medical insurance is still advised and is essential for all other visitors.

 Dental Services For urgent, out-of-hours dental treatment, contact the Central Medical Service (☎ 592 3434).

 Weather Even at the height of summer, temperatures in Amsterdam rarely get much above 25°C and are usually cooler. If you plan to do a lot of sightseeing on foot at this time, wear sunscreen and drink plenty of fluids – carry a bottle of mineral water rather than stopping at pavement terraces for beers. Rain is possible at all times, and winter temperatures occasionally drop low enough to freeze the canals.

 Drugs Prescription and non-prescription drugs and other medical products are sold in apotheeken (pharmacies), recognised by a green cross sign. The addresses of nearby out-of-hours pharmacies are posted on pharmacy doors or windows. Despite their name, *drogerijen* (drug stores) does not sell medicines, but toilet articles and cosmetics.

Safe Water Tap water is safe to drink all over the Netherlands. Bottled mineral water, often called by the generic name 'spa', after a popular Belgian label, is readily available in shops, restaurants and cafés.

CONCESSIONS

General
An Amsterdam Culture & Leisure Pass, which you can buy from NBT and VVV offices, allows free admission to more than 20 museums and attractions, as well as other free and discount offers.

Students/youths
An inexpensive Cultureel Jongeren Pas (Cultural Youth Pass), available from VVV offices or Uit Buro and valid for a year, entitles anyone under 26 to free admission to many museums, as well as to discounts on cultural performances and events.

Senior Citizens
Many museums, attractions and performance venues have reduced admission prices for seniors.

CLOTHING SIZES

Netherlands	UK	Rest of Europe	USA	
46	36	46	36	
48	38	48	38	
50	40	50	40	Suits
52	42	52	42	
54	44	54	44	
56	46	56	46	
41	7	41	8	
42	7.5	42	8.5	
43	8.5	43	9.5	
44	9.5	44	10.5	Shoes
45	10.5	45	11.5	
46	11	46	12	
37	14.5	37	14.5	
38	15	38	15	
39/40	15.5	39/40	15.5	
41	16	41	16	Shirts
42	16.5	42	16.5	
43	17	43	17	
34	8	34	6	
36	10	36	8	
38	12	38	10	
40	14	40	12	Dresses
42	16	42	14	
44	18	44	16	
38	4.5	38	6	
38	5	38	6.5	
39	5.5	39	7	
39	6	39	7.5	Shoes
40	6.5	40	8	
41	7	41	8.5	

WHEN DEPARTING

LANGUAGE

Most Dutch people speak at least some English and many are fluent. This can make it frustrating if you want to practise speaking Dutch, as often a question you ask in Dutch will be answered in English. Not everybody speaks English, though, making it useful to know some Dutch words, and attempts to use them will be appreciated. The 'oo' (pronounced 'oa' as in load) and 'ee' constructions (pronounced 'ay' as in day) are particularly problematic for English-speakers and lead to common errors; as an example, remember the department store Vroom & Dreesman is pronounced 'Vrome & Draysman'. If you pronounce 'ij' like English 'eye' you'll be close enough: for example *prijs* 'price'; *ontbijt* 'ontbite'.

hotel	*hotel*	breakfast	*ontbijt*
room	*kamer*	toilet	*toilet/WC*
single/	*eenpersoonskamer/*	bathroom	*badkamer*
double	*tweepersoonskamer*	shower	*douche*
one/two nights	*een/twee nachten*	balcony	*balkon*
per person/	*per persoon/*	key	*sleutel*
per room	*per kamer*	room service	*room service*
reservation	*reservering*	chambermaid	*kamermeisje*
rate	*prijs*		

bank	*bank*	American dollar	*Amerikaanse dollar*
exchange office	*wisselkantoor*	banknote	*papiergeld*
post office	*postkantoor*	coin	*wisselgeld/kleingeld*
cashier	*kassa*	credit card	*creditcard*
foreign exchange	*buitenlands geld*	traveller's cheque	*reischeque*
currency	*valuta*	exchange rate	*wisselkoers*
British pound	*Engels/Britse pond*	commission charge	*commissie*

restaurant	*restaurant*	starter	*voorgerecht*
café	*café*	main course	*hoofdgerecht*
table	*tafel*	dish of the day	*dagschotel*
menu	*menukaart*	dessert	*nagerecht*
set menu	*menu*	drink	*drank/drankje*
wine list	*wijnkaart*	waiter	*ober*
lunch	*lunch/middageten*	waitress	*serveerster*
dinner	*diner/avondeten*	the bill	*de rekening*

aeroplane	*vliegtuig*	single/return	*enkele reis/retour*
airport	*luchthaven*	first/	*eerste klas/*
train	*trein*	second class	*tweede klas*
station	*station*	ticket office	*boekingskantoor*
bus	*bus*	timetable	*dienstregeling*
station	*busstation*	seat	*plaats*
ferry	*veerboot*	non-smoking	*niet roken*
port	*haven*	reserved	*gereserveerd*
ticket	*reisekaart*	taxi!	*taxi!*

yes	*ja*	help!	*help!*
no	*nee*	today	*vandaag*
please	*alstublieft*	tomorrow	*morgen*
thank you	*dank u wel*	yesterday	*gisteren*
hello	*dag/hallo*	how much?	*hoeveel?*
goodbye	*dag/tot ziens*	expensive	*duur*
goodnight	*welterusten*	closed	*gesloten*
sorry	*excuseer/pardon*	open	*geopend*

·INDEX

Acknowledgements

The Automobile Association wishes to thank the following photographers and libraries for their assistance in the preparation of this book.

BRIDGEMAN ART LIBRARY 23b The Nightwatch, c.1642 (oil on canvas) by Rembrandt Harmensz. van Rijn (1606-69), Rijksmuseum, Amsterdam, Holland, 24b Van Gogh's Bedroom at Arles, 1888 (oil on canvas) by Vincent van Gogh (1853-90), Rijksmuseum Vincent Van Gogh, Amsterdam, The Netherlands; MARY EVANS PICTURE LIBRARY 10b, 11a, 11b; HULTON GETTY 14b; GEORGE MCDONALD 46; PICTOR INTERNATIONAL front cover (c) girl with tulips; PICTURES 80, 87, 89; EDDY POSTHUMA DE BOER 85, 90; SPECTRUM COLOUR LIBRARY 27b, 76, 78, 79, 82, 83; THEATRE INSTITUUT NEDERLAND 72b; WORLD PICTURES 81, 84, 88a, 88b; www.euro.ecb.int 119 (euro notes).

The remaining photographs are held in the Association's own library (AA PHOTO LIBRARY) and were taken by Ken Paterson with the exception of the following: Alex Kouprianoff 2, 5b, 13c, 15a, 16a, 17a, 18a, 19a, 20a, 21a, 22a, 23a, 24a, 25a, 26a, 43, 35, 36c, 43, 45, 50/51, 52b, 53b, 55b, 61b, 62b, 66b, 67b, 74/75, 91b, 122 a, 122b, 122c; Wyn Voysey front cover (a) clogs, 6a, 7a, 8a, 9a, 10a, 12a, 13a, 14a, 28, 29, 31, 34a, 36a, 38, 39a, 40, 41, 42a, 44a, 48a, 51a, 52a, 55a, 56a, 59a, 60a, 61a, 62a, 64a, 65a, 66a, 67a, 68a, 70a, 72a, 75a, 77, 91a, 92, 93, 94, 95, 96, 97, 98, 99, 100, 101, 102, 103, 104, 105, 106, 107, 108, 109, 110, 111, 112, 113, 114, 115, 116,

Page layout: Barfoot Design